FORGIVEN

... Finding Peace in the
Aftermath of Abortion

Christina Ryan Claypool

including "Mom's Story" by Glenna Mary Sprang

FORGIVEN

FIRST EDITION
Copyright © 2004 by
Christina Ryan Claypool

Library of Congress Catalog Card Number: 2003115862

Editors: Mike Lackey, JoAnne Koch Cramberg, Sean Lausé, Mary Lausé, and Larry Claypool
Cover Art and Graphics by Stan Myers
Cover Photo by Katie Garlock

ISBN 0-7880-2112-5

PRINTED IN U.S.A.

*Dedicated to the memory
of my beloved Cassie
and to the millions of other babies
who have been aborted,
and to their grieving mothers*

*"In Rama was there a voice heard, lamentation
and weeping, and great mourning, Rachel weeping for her children, and would not be comforted,
because they are not."* — Matthew 2:18 KJV

ABOUT THE COVER

In July of 2001, I was blessed to find that a resting place for my aborted baby existed in Restlawn Memorial Park in Grand Rapids, Michigan. The "Garden of Hope" was developed through a vision to design a place where post-abortive women and men could go to find comfort and ministry. The focal point of this spiritual park is a bronze sculpture created by nationally acclaimed artist, Beverly Paddleford. The "Hope" piece as it is referred to is a sculpture of Jesus holding an infant, with the baby's mother at Jesus' side.

Encouraged by Nancy Pruett, Director of Sav-a-life in Tupelo, Mississippi, I visited the "Garden of Hope" in Grand Rapids, since I had already planned a very similar portrait for this book's cover. Garden of Hope Project Director, Mary Verwys showed me a lovely artist's rendition of the sculpture created by Stan Myers.

My deepest appreciation is extended to the Lord's servants who allowed me to use this same rendition for *Forgiven's* cover. I pray that it provides you with the same sense of God's love and healing, as it ministers to me.

Due to the success of the Garden of Hope Memorial in Grand Rapids, other sites featuring the "Hope" piece have been created. These locations include: Tupelo, Mississippi — Austin, Texas — Cincinnati, Ohio — Timisoara, Romania, Lancaster, Pennsylvania, Bakersfield, California, Toronto, Canada (pending), Florence, Alabama (pending), and Naples, Florida, where a permanent home for the sculpture is yet to be found.

For information on placing a Garden of Hope in your area contact Beverly Paddleford at www.hopemonument.com or call Eagle Bronze Foundry at (307) 332-5436. Prints of the artist's rendition of the "Hope Piece" used for this cover are also available through www.gardenofhopememorial.org.

CONTENTS

FOREWORD

Dr. Mark I. Bubeck
President Emeritus,
International Center for Biblical Counseling

As a pastor counselor, I have witnessed the guilt and pain of abortion in the lives of numerous counselees. Counseling victims of abortion is never easy. As this book strongly illustrates, true healing from that guilt is only possible in the Lord Jesus Christ. I have also had some personal experience with the need for forgiveness.

Several decades ago, in the early years of my pastoral ministry, I made a terrible mistake. A Christian couple having marital problems came from another church to seek my counsel. Marital quarreling had left terrible wounds in both of their lives. As they unfolded their story, I realized that my youth and my lack of experience had not prepared me for their needs. I referred them on to a "Christian" psychiatrist who had greatly helped others I had sent to him. I was confident that he would be able to help them work through conflicts too great for me to handle. I was not prepared for what followed.

A major problem in the marriage had resulted after one of their frequent quarrels. The wife had fled the home, went to a bar, became intoxicated and was seduced by a man she met at the bar. That "one-night stand" resulted in pregnancy. Even though this was before the Supreme Court's Roe vs. Wade decision, the psychiatrist was advising abortion to solve this unwanted pregnancy. He assured the husband and wife that he could arrange it through the mental health hospital so that it would be entirely legal.

The husband was very pleased with such a solution. He wanted to be restored to his wife but not with her carrying another man's baby. The wife was not so sure. Her conscience was already troubling her. If she went through with this "solution" what would God think about it? She called me to gain my counsel about what she should do. I had not faced any problem like this in my seminary training, pastors' fellowship meetings or any other setting. After praying with her over the phone and talking with her about it at some length, I gave her some very wrong counsel. I reasoned that this was a "Christian" psychiatrist who surely knew what was best. If he felt this was the only way to give them a new start for their marriage and her husband was supporting such a decision, she should not feel guilty for taking their counsel and going through with an abortion.

How wrong my counsel was. The Lord disturbed me about my decision, but I brushed it off. My counseling training had led me to believe that good psychological counseling could solve most human emotional problems. I convinced myself that surely this fine, Christian psychiatric counselor could not be wrong. My conscience, however, was not convinced. I didn't sleep well. A few days later when I tried to call the lady to talk further about the matter, I discovered that the abortion had been completed. I knew that to talk to her further about my reservations would only complicate matters more. I had to live with my guilt. My guilt became even more severe when I later learned that the couple eventually divorced.

I realized too late that abortion is the taking of an innocent life. It produces "bloodguilt!" Bloodguilt, the taking of another human life, brings a guilt upon the one responsible for ending that life which is perhaps more devastating than any other kind of guilt.

I began to identify with the Old Testament character King David whose bloodguilt also pursued him. This experience is recorded in Psalm 51. His guilt came from the abuse of his power and authority in his vain attempt to cover his adulterous sin with Bathsheba. After Bathsheba became pregnant with David's child, David arranged for the murder of her husband, Uriah. **(II Samuel 11, 12)** David married Bathsheba and for a little season it seemed to work, but God sent Nathan the prophet to put His finger on David's murderous act. David's guilt for his sin overwhelmed him. One can feel his pain when he cries in broken repentance: *"Save me from bloodguilt, O God, the God who saves me, and my tongue will sing of your righteousness."* **(Psalm 51:14 NIV)**

It wasn't until many years later when I memorized Psalm 51 that I finally was able to find personal healing. As I prayed through the matter of my own bloodguilt in that counseling situation, the Lord helped me accept His cleansing and forgiveness. I found myself echoing the words of Psalmist David's cry: *"Save me from bloodguilt, O God, the God who saves me..."*

Relating to the reader my own personal story has helped me focus on the tremendous importance of this new book. As in no other account that I have read, Christina Ryan Claypool has been able to express the guilt and pain caused by abortion as it needs to be told. Her writing skill, her grasp of biblical truth, her compassion, and her loving understanding engulf the reader.

In relating the story of her own abortion, she has been able to communicate the agony of "bloodguilt" with convincing candor. Christina also relates some startling statistics in this book — concerning the number of women who have had abortions. If these statistics relate even a measure of the true picture, every pastor in every local church needs to make a book like this accessible and available to everyone in his congregation. One knows that this work will be like a "balm in Gilead" (Jeremiah 8:22) that God will use to help toward the healing of those wounded by abortion.

Dr. Bubeck is also the best-selling author of books including: *The Adversary, Overcoming The Adversary* and *Raising Lambs among Wolves*

FOREWORD

J. Kenneth Blackwell
Secretary of State of Ohio

Choices are a powerful component of the human saga. The choices we make, whether consciously or subconsciously, have the power to bless or curse, unite or divide, call forth love or hate, and seek or extend forgiveness. These dilemmas play themselves out daily on the human stage, and thus, shape a person's character — be it good or bad.

Because of our human condition, all of us are prone to make poor choices that bring condemnation and judgment on ourselves and pain to others. Such is the story of Christina Ryan Claypool. In an incredibly vulnerable and courageous spirit, Christina lays out the aftermath and consequences of a decision that has shaped her in ways imaginable only to God. As Christina takes us through her healing process, two things become evident. One, nothing is wasted. God allowed, or maybe more correctly, God directed other events and people to come into Christina's life to assist in her healing process. Through a woman acknowledging her own grieving process over a lost child in a laundromat, Christina recognized the need to give herself permission to grieve. The second truth, one that is similar in all of our histories, is if we will quiet ourselves long enough so we can acknowledge and observe goodness being done on our behalf, we will realize the profound fact that grace is everywhere.

The fact that God's grace is present and available to each one of us no matter what our circumstances, ironically, is the other side of nothing being wasted in our lives. Our great hope is that in our moments of imperfection, somehow and in some way, God is for us and demonstrates His love for us no matter what we have done. If we believe this, then it is also plausible to believe God wishes to demonstrate his love for us through any means possible to get our attention.

The question for each of us, answered so victoriously by Christina, is whether the fallout and consequences of our choices will block us from receiving the love of God, and therefore, prevent healing to occur from our personal, self-made concentration camps.

For a woman, man or family member now struggling through the post abortive process, how does one find, let alone dream of, a glorious freedom? Self-hatred is prevalent. Regret is rampant. Isolation is evident. Recovering alcoholic and author, Brennan Manning, notes, "Unhealthy guilt is self-centered; it stirs our emotions to churn in self-destructive ways, leads to depression and despair, closes us in upon ourselves and preempts the presence of a compassionate God."

Christina's story reveals wanderings amidst her desire for wholeness and peace. It is that example that gives all of us, but specifically those who are wrestling with the abortion experience, hope for a preferred future. How amazing that in the midst of, and in spite of her shame, a real and an abiding peace came. In his book *Shame and Grace*, Lewis Smedes writes, "Am I not more in tune with realty if I accept my shame as the cost of failing to be the self I ought to be, the self I am meant to be, and the self I really want to be? This is healthy shame, and we are closest to health when we let ourselves feel the pain of it and be led by the pain to do something about it."

How well this articulates Christina's transformation. For the reader who is drawn to these pages due to a similar set of circumstances, I offer you Christina's example and pray your pain, of all things, may lead you in a manner and on a path that brings God's love to you at your point of need.

The Honorable J. Kenneth Blackwell is the Secretary of State of Ohio. He is well known for championing the rights of all people including the post-abortive and the unborn.

INTRODUCTION

If you are reading this, you or someone you love has probably been a victim of either a surgical or medical abortion. Abortion, which is "one of the most common surgical procedures in the United States,"(1) has left many men and women with guilt and grief that time alone cannot heal.

In my first book, *Victory over Suffering,* I record the steps God used to heal me of the abuse I suffered as a child. That book was easier to write as it was about someone else's sin. This book is about my tragic decision to abort a child, my ignorance, and the aftermath of suffering that was left in my life. It is also about the grace of God and the steps of healing which He has so mercifully provided.

If you have never experienced the trauma of abortion, you might not understand why I use the word "victim" to describe the participants in this devastating act. Only those of us who have either made the erroneous decision to have an abortion, or encouraged someone we love to make this choice, know the weighty price we pay for our mistake.

I ask you to read this book with an open heart. According to a study by the Alan Guttmacher Institute, one out of every six women within the evangelical church has had an abortion. (2)

Later statistics from this same organization indicate that of the women surveyed who have had abortions — 42.8% identify themselves as Protestant, while 27.4% claim to be Catholic. Only 22.2% of the women involved in this research reported that they had no religious affiliation at all. (3)

The women responding to this survey do not look like common criminals. Any one of them could be the lady sitting next to you in the church pew on Sunday attired in a sophisticated outfit, with a smile on her face.

You cannot see her scars or hear her desperate cries for help and forgiveness because her shame and the fear of judgment

silence her. She does not believe that she is entitled to help, as she
knows that she murdered the life she was entrusted to carry. She
did not realize in the desperation of her poor decision that she was
killing her baby, but she recognizes it in the pain of the aftermath.
One of the greatest traumas of abortion is the isolation of the
grieving. You do not expect to grieve, and you feel you have no
right to grieve, so you are unprepared for the enormity of the pain.

I lived in this isolation for over a decade, too ashamed to tell
anyone that I needed help — including my pro-life mother.

As I worked on this manuscript, I finally confessed the abortion to mom and asked for her support. Her contribution of Chapter Nine, "Mom's Story" was birthed. I did not realize that the
miscarriage my mother had experienced as a young woman was
the catalyst for her involvement in the pro-life movement. She
also experienced the trauma of a crisis pregnancy and the devastating grief that miscarriage brought into her life. She funneled the
pain that her loss created into zeal to reach others in the midst of a
crisis pregnancy.

Like my mother, I have also suffered the physically frightening and emotionally painful experience of a first trimester miscarriage. A large number of women have chosen a medical abortion
through the use of the abortion pill mifepristone (RU-486) since
the September 2001 FDA approval of the drug. (4) My heart breaks
for them and for their aborted children.

Only a woman who has personally experienced the trauma of
miscarriage can be an accurate representative for what these women
have experienced under the guise of an abortion in the privacy of
their own home. "What the manufacturer of mifepristone refers to
only as a side effect of "bleeding that is sometimes heavier than
menses"(5) will actually be a visible reminder of the baby they
chose to abort. Complications from this drug have also been reported to be responsible for the deaths of young women.

I cannot erase the memory of my own poor choice either, but
my desire is to turn my trauma from abortion into a balm for the
healing of others. I am writing this book for the thousands who are
still hurting, for the innocent unborn who deserve the gift of life,

and for my daughter Cassie who never had the opportunity to live because I did not allow it.

Her life ended in one traumatic moment in an Akron abortion clinic when she was violently ripped from my womb. For over a decade, I dreamed of my baby being torn apart limb-by-limb, and I grieved and hated myself for what I'd done. After years of self-torment, I have accepted that I cannot change what has happened. Yet, God promises that He will create good from every evil that comes in our lives.

I found Jesus Christ as my agony drove me to the Cross. I was able to rationalize every sin prior to my abortion, but the unexpected remorse led me to a loving Savior who continues to heal me in the most miraculous of ways.

There are eight specific steps to healing listed in this book. Pain often accompanies the healing process, but God will be there for you at each step, just as He has been there for me.

God's foremost desire is to spare the lives of the innocent unborn in order to prevent their mothers from experiencing the grievous wound abortion causes. He also desires to heal those who are post-abortive and to educate the church on how to reach this hurting population. I pray His blessing upon you as you seek the wholeness you will experience in His forgiving arms. I pray also that God will call a generation of compassionate clergy and wounded healers who are willing to expose their scars to stop the mass slaughter of our children.

Christina

CHAPTER ONE

REMEMBERING A PAINFUL PAST

Today I'm a Christian speaker and author, as well as being a wife and a mother. Some people have read the autobiographical book I've written about abuse. *Victory over Suffering* has been promoted on several national television programs. The book is about the victory that God has given me after suffering a troubled childhood.

It was especially difficult to share about sexual abuse as the stigma of this abuse left me feeling tainted and dirty. As a young woman, my reaction to the abuse led me on a self-destructive path that resulted in suicide attempts and years of hospitalizations for "mental problems."

Even after I gave my life to Jesus Christ on a psychiatric ward in 1986, my self-esteem was non-existent. If it were not for God's direction, I would not have documented my past struggles. He showed me quite clearly that by writing my first book, I would heal, and others would be set free.

At first when I shared about the abuse, and the years I'd spent living in and out of mental wards, it was terrifying. Then it became a part of everyday life for me. So much so, that at one point God had to sternly remind me to be compassionate and patient with those who were only beginning to disclose about the abuse they had endured. With abuse, I was the victim, but with abortion, now that was a different matter, or so I thought.

On December 3, 1983, I had an abortion that only a handful of what I thought were very trustworthy people knew about. My own mother and best friends didn't know about this hidden secret. I was too ashamed to tell others that I had once been involved in a casual relationship that had resulted in an unplanned pregnancy. In retrospect, I don't think anyone except God knew the price I had paid for hiding my shame and guilt.

To outward observers, I appeared to have it all together. In some ways, as long as no one knew about my secret sin, I could deceive myself into thinking that my image was intact. I believed that God could use someone like me who had been abused, lived in mental hospitals, had been drug-addicted and suffered the pain of divorce. Yet, I was convinced that God could not use someone who had an abortion.

There were times I stood and listened as Christians told me about the despicable women who had committed the sin of abortion. I remember one specific incident when a woman I greatly admired shared how she could never feel the same about someone who had an abortion. She didn't know she was talking to one of those someones. There were occasions when people would tell me how angry they were with women who had aborted their babies when they or someone they loved longed for a child. I understood that anger. I directed it at myself for years.

Then I met Katie. Katie was a vivacious brunette with a zeal and purity that seemed like a breath of fresh air. We met a few years ago, when our paths crossed through the Christian television station where I worked as a producer/reporter for a daily ministry program. I attended a worship service for people in full-time ministry and Katie was there. Like me, Katie appeared to have it all together. But she too had a hidden secret.

During the worship service, those in attendance were invited to come forth and share a testimony. Katie slowly took the long walk to the front. She began to share about a life that had been very troubled. I thought of her as the perfect wife and mother and ministry worker. I assumed she'd grown up in a Christian home and never strayed.

Katie talked about rebellious teenage years, about knowing God but not serving Him and becoming involved in a promiscuous lifestyle. While still a teen, Katie found herself pregnant.

Because she felt she couldn't let anyone know, abortion seemed to be her only choice. Katie's voice cracked as she shared her story. Tears streamed down her pretty face.

Horrified, I sat rigid in my seat. I remember thinking, *"Be quiet, Katie, they'll all hate you. Why are you doing this to yourself? There is no mercy or forgiveness for you. Abortion is the unpardonable sin."*

To my surprise no one began to throw stones at Katie. I think someone even reached out to hug her. Katie's testimony prompted another young woman who was there to share her sad story. She had grown up in a family in ministry. When she found herself single and pregnant, it was more than she thought she could bear. She wept as she told how she also opted for abortion.

In the weeks that followed I watched to see if Katie's position in ministry would be taken from her, or if she would be treated differently. In contrast, God only seemed to bless her more for her courage to share her past.

People said they thought of me as being confident and assertive. Yet, gentle Katie had taught me an important lesson about the power of speaking the truth. I witnessed that your world didn't fall apart if you talked about abortion. Not only did your world not fall apart, but honesty was the key that opened the doors for others to disclose, too. After all, Jesus said, **"You will know the truth and the truth shall make you free." (John 8:32 KJV)**

Katie's disclosure gave me so much courage that I decided to ask my supervisor if we could do a weeklong series on abortion. He said the topic probably would be better confined to just one segment, rather than an entire week of shows.

I felt strongly that God wanted to heal women in our audience who were hurting from the aftermath of abortion. God also wanted to prevent others from taking the lives of their unborn children and ending up with an unbearable grief. I was not ready to share that I was one of the women who needed help. If I could have, I'm sure my boss would have better understood my passion for this cause.

Although I was disappointed, I knew I must accept his decision to do only one feature. I searched for the most healing testimony that I could find. I discovered several very moving stories, and it was difficult to choose just one. As always, God works in mysterious ways to accomplish His will when we ask for His help.

One day while I was on the phone with a prospective guest, I said matter-of-factly, "One out of six women in the church has had an abortion."(1) I remember my boss glancing at me in a very strange way as he overheard that conversation. I don't think he realized the enormity of this problem within the church community. These statistics, which had initially shocked me, too, caused my manager to change his mind about the relevance of the topic of abortion.

A few weeks later, he announced that I was to begin working on a weeklong series concerning abortion. This was not an easy task, since my own past made delving into the abortion issue more difficult than I had anticipated.

I started to interview prospective guests whose lives had been affected by abortion. One woman had been told that she needed to have an abortion for medical reasons. Her doctor did not feel she was healthy enough to carry another child. She was a strong Christian, so even though her doctor's words caused fear to enter her heart, she knew abortion was not an option. Today, this woman has a beautiful teenage daughter who would have been aborted if her mother had followed the doctor's advice.

My experience with doctors had been strangely similar. Interviewing this guest made a flood of memories return for me. Suddenly, I was transported back almost fifteen years to the events leading up to the birth of my son.

Because of the emotional imbalance in my early life, my attending psychiatrist at that time felt I should never have children. The doctor believed strongly that a tubal ligation should be done to ensure that I did not get pregnant. Because I was so young, only in my mid-twenties, the signature of another physician was required before this procedure could be performed.

There was a possibility that a failed suicide attempt had caused me to miscarry a child in my early twenties. I thought it was for the best because everyone close to me had convinced me that I would not be a good mother.

My doctor sincerely believed the stress of motherhood would be too much for a woman in my mental state. Despite his prognosis the signature of another physician could not be secured.

At 25, I had an exploratory female surgery called a laparoscopy. Following the surgery, the gynecologist came to my hospital room and said there was a great deal of scar tissue in my organs. With compassion, he explained to me that children would probably not be a part of my future.

I didn't care. I didn't think I would be a good mother anyway. I was almost relieved at the news; therefore tying my tubes wouldn't be necessary. Yet, I did not understand why I felt that I had just been given a life sentence.

A few months later, I met a man who was confused like I was. We were both loners who used drugs to mask our different kinds of pain. We moved into an apartment together and began to "play house." Things didn't go very well, **"for the wages of sin is death."** (**Romans 6:23 KJV**) Death came to our unrighteous relationship rather quickly. We hadn't worried about protecting against pregnancy, since I thought I wasn't able to have children anyway.

Despite my unstable romantic relationship, I was doing pretty well for the first time in my life. I had one year of college left to complete, and even though I didn't have a degree, I had been determined to become a newspaper reporter.

To make the dream of becoming a journalist a reality, I sat in the local newspaper's waiting area for three consecutive days. I was hoping to get an opportunity to talk with someone about a job. On the third day, the publisher reluctantly agreed to see me. I convinced him to give me a chance at reporting. Finally, I had a job that made me feel good about myself.

My chaotic romance ended as the new job began — with my boyfriend moving out of our apartment. I threw myself into being an associate editor at the small newspaper. Then I started getting sick in the mornings.

My symptoms weren't life threatening, but I was miserable. I had to go to the bathroom all the time, and I was nauseous. I went to my family physician and he told me he thought I had a bladder infection. He gave me an antibiotic to take care of the infection, and sent me home.

The next couple weeks, I felt even worse. I could hardly eat anything without feeling sick. I had little energy, so working my usual 12 to 14 hour days had become almost impossible. I could barely get out of bed and I felt like I was pregnant.

I called the doctor and told him of my suspicion, but he assured me that pregnancy wasn't a possibility in my case. In frustration I purchased a home pregnancy test and sure enough, the result was positive.

Part of me was overjoyed; the woman who was never going to be able to have children was pregnant! But I was also terrified. With my boyfriend gone, I was alone and afraid. I knew that a baby would not be healthy for me emotionally. How could I be so sure of this? My psychiatrist had told me so.

In panic, I called my family doctor and told him the test was positive. He still did not believe it. He sent me to the hospital to have another test.

I went to his office for the test results. My family physician walked into the examining room appearing embarrassed and contrite. He timidly mumbled, "Doctors are human beings. We make mistakes."

I knew right away. "I'm pregnant, aren't I?"

He looked up and nodded. *I couldn't be pregnant — it had to go away*. After all, the psychiatrist had warned that having a child would be too much for me.

I became hysterical and the feeling of being trapped began to settle in. I pleaded with my doctor asking for his help. I frantically said, "This can't be happening because I'm not strong enough to deal with this problem. You have to make it go away."

He looked at me very sternly and let me know that I was carrying a baby and he wasn't going to do anything to help my problem go away. I would have to find another kind of doctor if I wanted that. (In later years, I felt immensely grateful to this physician, as his reaction probably saved my son's life.) This doctor did not deliver babies, so he referred me to a group of family physicians who did.

I called my baby's father and told him I was pregnant. Our parents had grown up together and had been friends for years. Since this was decades ago, my baby's dad did the noble thing and suggested that we get married. Much to the relief of our parents, we married a few weeks later, but it was a marriage doomed to failure.

We both felt trapped by circumstance and unwanted responsibility. We had not known how to get along before; adding the prospect of a baby to the picture definitely didn't help. I was so physically ill that I had to quit my job. Without an income, I became completely financially dependent on my new husband, which terrified me.

At four months pregnant, I went for my scheduled checkup. The regular doctor wasn't there. The physician filling in for him could see that I was very distraught and listened to my story. In his hand was my chart, which listed my mental and physical history, including my multiple suicide attempts. The substitute physician looked at me with great compassion and said, "You don't have to have this baby."

At first, I thought I misunderstood the doctor. Then he made it clear that because of my emotional condition, it might be best to terminate my pregnancy. Without using the word, he suggested that an abortion might be a wise decision.

But I had already fought for my baby's life. A few days after our forced wedding, I had started bleeding. My regular physician thought I had lost the baby. When we found out later that I hadn't, I felt my first feelings of maternal protection. *Nobody was taking my baby from me now*!

Zachary Scott Ryan was born on January 6, 1981, with the director of the local women's shelter at my side. There was no adoring husband to hold my hand, or brightly decorated nursery awaiting Zach's arrival. I didn't even know what to name him. A kind nurse read a book with boys' names to me. When she reached the last letter of the alphabet, I thought I better choose a name. "Zachary" sounded like a good choice to me. I had no idea at the time that the name's original meaning is "Jehovah remembered."

God had remembered me with a beautiful eight-pound boy with dark hair and blue eyes. He was the first baby born from the women's shelter in our county. The shelter was the only place I had to go when Zachary's dad left me. I was about seven months pregnant at the time and the strain of our pressure-ridden marriage finally took its toll. As I had feared, now I was truly alone and without any financial support.

After my baby was born I wasn't alone anymore. I had Zachary to take care of and like many single moms, I made a decision to do whatever I needed to take care of my baby. We were going to be okay. I would see to that. I resolved to never be dependent on any man again.

However, I did mentally catalogue the doctor's advice, when he suggested abortion as an answer for someone with an emotional balance as precarious as mine. It was the catalyst for the decision I would make years later. I didn't have to have a baby. At that time, I wasn't a Christian like the lady in the story who didn't listen to her doctor's advice to abort her baby for health reasons. I didn't know I had a God willing to take care of my little boy and me. I thought I only had myself. I was going to make sure that we made it — no matter what.

CHAPTER TWO

DEADLY CONSEQUENCES

After my son was born in 1981, I returned to school. A year and a half later I graduated from Bluffton College with a B.A. in Business Administration/English minor. Having a degree was very affirming for a single mother on public assistance, who had spent the past ten years in and out of mental hospitals.

I think being on welfare bothered me more than the stigma of mental illness. When Zachary's dad left, I was seven months pregnant. We were young and pregnancy was the only reason we married. It wasn't surprising a few months after our forced wedding, when he packed his things and headed out West to find himself, leaving me penniless. Early in the pregnancy I had to quit my stress-filled reporter's job, because my morning sickness was so severe.

I tried to find a new job after my husband left, but employers would look at my big belly and shake their heads. With no source of income, living in a woman's shelter on welfare became my only option. The shelter was actually a four-bedroom home overcrowded with women and children who had in some way been abused or abandoned. There was a kind of hopelessness that permeated the place. This was emotionally devastating for a young woman who had prided herself on being middle class.

My maternal grandmother came and rescued us from the shelter a week after Zachary was born. She took us into her home for the first few months of his life, until I could find a government-subsidized apartment. Before he was born, she had been angry with me for the mess I had created. But after she saw her chubby blue-eyed great-grandson, she fell in love with him.

Grandma insisted that I finish college, so that I would have greater opportunities to take care of Zachary and myself. She bought Zach's diapers for the next two years, and sometimes watched him so I could attend classes. Even with her help and my welfare benefits, there was not enough money, not even for necessities.

Despite my bleak circumstances, there seemed to be a core of steel that had been implanted within me at Zach's birth. I was determined to succeed. I maintained an honors grade point average, and began to write again. The local paper printed my news stories and the college gave me academic credit for my writing.

I compartmentalized my life, and was diligent about completing tasks. I used prescription drugs and marijuana as a form of medication to manage my emotional pain, not realizing that my lifestyle was adding to my trauma.

For six months following graduation, I couldn't find work. It was 1982 and the recession was in full swing. The stress of living in a tiny apartment with a toddler — with no money and little hope for the future was frightening. I was heading down the wrong path since my drug use was steadily escalating. I desperately wanted to take care of Zach, but it seemed to be a losing battle.

One morning sobbing about the situation, I asked God for help. I didn't even know if God was real. If He was, I didn't think He would hear me. Years earlier, while living through a childhood plagued by abuse, I had begged God for help. It seemed that God had ignored my plea then, because no help came. But maybe God would answer for Zachary's sake, as Zach wasn't tarnished like me — at least that's what I erroneously thought.

A few days later, a large tobacco corporation granted me an interview. Miraculously, within 24 hours they offered me what seemed to be a dream job to a single mom on welfare. The days of struggle were over. With my new company car, leather briefcase and expense account, I became an instant success.

For almost a year I climbed the corporate ladder. Then my reckless lifestyle caught up with me. I was experiencing symptoms of pregnancy for the second time in three years. I couldn't believe that I might be pregnant again since my life was just beginning to come together. Terrified by what appeared to be a hopeless situation, I scheduled an appointment for an abortion.

It was Dec. 3, 1983. I did not realize it then, but it was a day that would change my life forever. It was a cold, blustery morning.

I awoke with a feeling of desperation, but I didn't have time for desperation. I had to hurry, because my best friend, Alan, would arrive soon. Alan was in love with me, but I wasn't in love with him. Therefore, he settled for whatever part of my life I allowed him to share. Today, it was to drive me to an abortion clinic to help get rid of a baby that belonged to another man.

I pulled on my clothes, an old pair of blue jeans and a burgundy sweater. I felt bloated and sick. My blue eyes had dark circles underneath. I was 29 years old, but when I looked into the mirror, I looked like a frightened child. I had been escaping my problems with drugs and alcohol, but they weren't helping now. The alcohol made me sick, and marijuana was no cure for an unwanted pregnancy.

I wasn't sure I was pregnant, but I was nauseous and had missed a couple of periods, and I was tired all the time. I had all the symptoms of pregnancy that I had with my son who would soon celebrate his third birthday. I hadn't taken a test or gone for pre-natal care as there wasn't going to be a need for that. I was going to take care of this unwanted glob of tissue my way.

My stoic German grandmother had finally forgiven me for my first mistake, and was even proud of the successful businesswoman I had become. I resolved in my heart that I would rather die than tell her I was pregnant again.

I looked at Zachary, my sweet little boy, who was finally going to have some of the things I thought he needed. He didn't need a brother or sister. I couldn't look at it that way I told myself. I had to keep convincing myself that this was only a glob of tissue.

My boyfriend and I were both products of the sexual revolution. We had a casual relationship without commitment. He was an insurance executive; young and upwardly mobile just like me. The night we conceived, we were drinking and getting high, and my birth control failed. When I called to tell him what had happened, he said, "I'm sorry, let me know if there is anything I can do."

The tone of his voice was reserved and professional. I had made a mistake calling him — there had been no commitment.

What was I thinking? Immediately I started hating him with great intensity and blaming him for what I must now face alone.

The knock at the door interrupted my thoughts. Alan stood there looking nervous and cold. "Let's go. We have a couple of hundred miles to drive and the roads aren't great," he said. We drove about halfway and even though I was feeling sick, we stopped at a restaurant. By this time, I was so nervous that I couldn't hold a glass in my trembling hands. I managed to spill ice water all over the restaurant's tiled floor. We drove the last hundred miles to the Akron abortion clinic in silence.

A few years earlier I had gone to college in Akron. I still had friends there and I was going to need all the moral support I could get. I looked out the car window at a picket line, and what seemed like an angry mob.

It was such a traumatic time that my memory is still very blurred. Yet, I will never forget the condemning signs or the shouts of incrimination directed at me. I also remember one other thing; not one person in the crowd of demonstrators offered to help me. No one approached and offered me a place to stay until the baby was born, or to help with the medical bills. I heard yelling and jeering but no one asked if they could have the baby I was about to abort.

Within moments, Alan whisked me past the crowd, and we were safely inside the clinic. The waiting room was filled with young women. Some were nervously laughing, while others were crying. Despite the large number of females, there were only a few men present to offer support.

A young blonde woman who looked like a college student was weeping and clinging tightly to her boyfriend. He kept comforting her and reassuring her it was going to be okay.

I checked in at the desk. The lady asked me the reason for my visit. I just assumed they would know. I didn't want to say the word out loud. I stammered and then handed her my money order for the procedure. She looked at the other receptionist and giggled. Her behavior was so unprofessional and condescending that I wanted to turn around and run away, but I didn't.

By this time, my friend from college days, Alicia, had arrived. She had an abortion a few years earlier, and she seemed fine. I'd called her and asked for a shoulder to lean on. The first thing she said when she saw me was, "Boy, do you look chubby."

Since I looked pregnant, I concluded that it must be true. Even though there hadn't been a test, I knew Alicia's remark confirmed my fear. Besides, I couldn't take a test this time. If the test revealed that I was carrying a baby, then I couldn't do this. I couldn't kill a baby, but I rationalized that I could get rid of some unwanted tissue. It had been too traumatic being pregnant and alone. I couldn't bear the thought of going through that again, so adoption seemed impossible, too.

Alan said he needed to disappear for a few hours. I knew he was heading for a local bar because his nerves were getting the best of him. After a brief wait, I was taken to another holding room in the back of the clinic. A couple girls callously talked about shopping when their procedure was over. There were others in the room still weeping. As I recall, most of them seemed like me, numb and unfeeling.

I walked down a hallway to the examining room. A young woman who had just finished her "procedure" was standing in the doorway. She had long brown hair that was thick and curly, and huge brown eyes. Her eyes had an empty gaze that haunts me to this day. Everything within me screamed, "Run." I knew something terrible had happened to that girl, but in my numbness it seemed too late to run. Devoid of emotion, I let myself be led into a small room where my baby's life was to end.

To my great astonishment, the technician who reached out to hold my hand as the doctor started the abortion had once been my neighbor. She had been arrested for dealing drugs and the last I knew she was in prison. But here she was. So much for confidentiality, so much for trained technicians — unless this was part of her rehabilitation.

I had not expected the pain or the sound the machine made as it sucked the tiny life out of my womb. I was surprised that it was over in a few minutes.

They took me to a follow-up room, and told me to take the prescription I would need to guard against infection. The attendant asked if I used birth control. I told her the kind I had been using. She nodded and said, "A lot of women have gotten pregnant using that particular product."

As she spoke, I felt light-headed and sick, but I had to know. "How far along was I?"

"About eight weeks," she said.

"*Oh, no, it's really happened, I've just killed my baby,*" I thought. Not only had I been pregnant, now it was documented on a clinical file that I was responsible for ending my child's life. I needed a drink, and so I asked if it would be okay to drink alcohol before I began taking the medication. The nurse assured me it would be okay just for tonight.

When Alan returned to the clinic to pick me up, he looked visibly relieved that it was over. He drove me to a bar where I drank scotch on the rocks, but nothing numbed the torment that was settling in my soul. In my guilt, I cursed my baby's father, but deep inside I knew it was my fault. It was my decision to sleep with a man I barely knew. Not realizing that decision would require me to pay a terrible price for the rest of my life.

The gravity of my mistake was on my mind while we were driving home from the clinic. About halfway into our trip there was a freak accident. The roads were snow-covered and slippery; and visibility was bad. A car came out of nowhere and forced us off the road. Alan, who was drunk at the time, was driving 60 miles an hour when the accident occurred. Despite his drunken state, he managed to maneuver the car to safety.

We had almost been killed, and for the first time in my life I realized that if I died I would have gone to Hell. I had never thought about Hell before. My life circumstances had been so bad that I used to jokingly say, "Earth is Hell."

In that split second I remembered my religious upbringing, which had taught me that Hell was real. The fact that it was a place of eternal torment, and that I had just been spared from going there was a sobering thought. I also sensed that somehow divine intervention had prevented the accident in order to give me more time — more time for what? I didn't know.

I went home and cried like I had not cried in years. I had a handmade clown named CoCo that a friend had given me. I talked to CoCo and poured my heart out to a wooden clown incapable of responding with comforting words. There was to be no healing — only more torment. I did not know how to turn to the God who had spared my life that night.

In the days following the abortion, I worked excessively to numb the pain. I was in a management-training program that caused me to blossom into a full-blown workaholic. By night, I retreated into the world of alcohol and drugs. I referred to marijuana as my medication. I would light a joint the moment I arrived home from work.

I was also required to travel extensively for my job. Many nights found me sleeping in hotels in strange cities. I hated to be away from Zach, so I squandered countless nights in hotel bars, subsequently waking up hung-over.

I did the best I could to take care of my little boy, who was growing rapidly. I really didn't know how to love, but he was beginning to teach me. He was always there with a smile or a hug, or a "Mommy, I love you" when I least deserved it. He loved me unconditionally even when my behavior did not warrant love. Having grown up in an alcoholic and abusive home, I did not want to repeat the cycle. But ironically I was doing just that. Sometimes, I would rage without provocation, and I know my temper must have frightened him.

One night I was so high, my son became terrified. He was only three or four years old, yet he insisted I call and get a relative to help us. Seeing my child's fear and lack of security was a sobering experience for me. I was desperate to change his life and mine, but I didn't know how.

I decided I needed to get married and settle down. I wanted to stop the destructive cycle that was going nowhere and find the real thing. I didn't know that Jesus Christ was the real thing, so I looked for a substitute.

I met a man who was on his way to a successful future. He was fun to be with and a very astute businessman. This looked like it could be a "happy-ever-after thing." We dated for a year or two, and I started talking about the future. I wanted a baby, and a little house with a white picket fence surrounded by red roses, and a gold wedding band.

The "man of my dreams" had a son years earlier, and then decided not to have more children. He knew about my abortion, but it was something we didn't talk about.

One night my boyfriend and I had a terrible argument. I was crying about wanting to get married and have a baby. I thought I needed a baby to take away the guilt I'd experienced since my abortion. I've since learned that the desire for an "atonement baby" is normal for most post-abortive women. Because I only realized this on a subconscious level, I couldn't express the reason for my need to my boyfriend. My grief had become unbearable, instead of getting better, the guilt was getting worse.

In frustration, I said, "Wouldn't you like to have a cute little girl with brown hair and big brown eyes who looks just like you?" I could tell by the look on his face that he was fed up with my intense need for a child. A need, he definitely did not share.

As he walked out the door, he said accusingly, "You murdered your baby."

Hearing that statement from someone who was supposed to love me was horrifying. I didn't understand that my boyfriend was just being cruel as an excuse to avoid commitment. My lifelong struggle with low self-esteem made me regard his words as true. The condemnation and judgment I lived with daily seemed justified. I was a murderer; therefore I had no right to enjoy a future filled with more children, or anything else good. Following this incident with my boyfriend, my self-destructive behavior escalated.

A friend from college days realized how deeply troubled I had become. My battle with addiction and mental illness had left me with the emotional maturity of someone in their teens, even though I had chronologically reached my thirties.

My friend Barb invited me to her church for a Sunday service. Normally, I stayed in bed until noon on Sunday, sleeping off a hangover induced by too much Scotch and marijuana. One beautiful summer Sunday morning, however, I put on a pretty white dress and went to church with her. To those in the church, I might have seemed as pure as my pristine white dress, but inside I felt dirty and alone.

At the pastor's invitation I went to the altar to pray, but no one, not even Barb, came to pray with me. There wasn't anyone to tell me that I needed a personal relationship with Jesus Christ; and that only through that relationship could I receive forgiveness. Instead, I naively prayed that God would give me the man I had been dating for my husband. I'm ashamed to say that I was addicted to him. I couldn't let him go, even though he was still angry with me for wanting a baby. At the time, I didn't know how to pray for God's will and to trust that He knew best.

A few weeks later, a woman from the church named Betty visited my home. Although, church often made me feel worse, I continued to attend, hoping to find some kind of answer. I still believed that my abortion was a sin beyond God's forgiveness.

That evening Betty and I sat at my kitchen table and talked. I felt so comfortable with her. She was a pretty woman with a very gentle spirit. Few people knew about my abortion, but I felt compelled to tell Betty. I shamefully explained to her, why God couldn't forgive me, and let her know just what an awful person I was. I didn't think there could be anyone in that church guilty of the horrible thing I had done.

Betty's reaction was not at all what I expected. She said very calmly, "I had an abortion, too." I was shocked at her confession, but relief flooded over me like waves. If God could forgive Betty, maybe He could forgive me, too. Shortly after Betty's only visit, she moved out west. Despite the fact that I would never see her again, Betty left me with my first glimmer of hope.

I also kept hoping that the man that I thought I was in love with would come back into my life. After we argued, he didn't contact me for months. Even though he had called me a murderer, and was insistent that we would have no more children, my addiction to him made me desperate. Eventually he returned, and we finally became engaged. Knowing my boundaries, I decided I could never discuss the possibility of a baby with him. I didn't know that deep inside; he had a great sense of morality about the sanctity of life. Despite the way we lived, I later found out that he thought abortion was very wrong.

I now understand his conviction despite the fact that before my abortion I had openly supported the pro-choice movement. I was very vocal about what I believed was a woman's right to choose. In my misguided zeal, I proudly had my name published in the local newspaper as being a supporter of pro-choice. My liberal friends complimented me for the courage of my commitment.

After my own abortion, my opinion changed. I began to realize the terrible consequences that resulted from what is portrayed as a harmless procedure. One of the consequences I experienced actually occurred while I was working as a corporate representative for a large manufacturer. One of the responsibilities of my job required that I spend lots of time checking product in supermarkets.

Following the abortion, it seemed like these stores were suddenly filled with babies. I would stare at them in sadness and think, "This is how old my baby would have been."

Whenever I thought about my aborted baby, I somehow sensed that it had been a girl. I had always wanted a daughter. I visualized that she had dark hair and brown eyes. I couldn't think about her for very long, because the next step to my mental vision was watching her being torn apart limb-by-limb.

My torment overcame me one afternoon in a grocery store when a young mother slapped her baby daughter in the mouth for crying. I became hysterical and begged the cashier to call someone to report the woman. I knew I hadn't protected my child; I felt I had to protect this baby that appeared to be only eight months old. The cashier told me very sharply, "Pull yourself together. There's nothing we can do." I wasn't capable of pulling myself together. At the time, what I didn't realize was that I was on the verge of having a nervous breakdown.

My mind began to lose touch with reality. Sometimes at night when I was alone, I thought I heard a baby crying. It was a faint, faraway sound with a haunting echo that tormented me. Scotch and pot muffled the sound, but it was still there.

Outwardly, my life looked like a success. I was advancing with the corporation, going to graduate school at night, and was finally engaged to the man I had asked God to give me — Mr. Wonderful. But things weren't so wonderful.

Despite the fact that Zachary was a fun-loving five-year-old, even his love couldn't stop my pain. I had lived for Zach, but I was beginning to believe the lie that he would be better off if I wasn't around.

It had been almost three years since the abortion, and I didn't want to live anymore. Not only had I killed my baby, now I was thinking about killing myself.

CHAPTER THREE

THE CONVERSION

"God not only Saves, He Restores."

I didn't kill myself, but in the fall of 1986 I had to be hospitalized. I hadn't been confined to a mental ward for almost a decade, but my life had spiraled out of control. I was a corporate representative with a college degree, a relationship that appeared perfect, a nice home and a beautiful son. What was wrong with me?

My sin had found me out. Years of wrong living and pursuing self-indulgent values had taken their toll. There was a root issue inside of me that had never been healed.

A childhood traumatized by the pain of sexual abuse had led to several near-fatal suicide attempts. I had already been hospitalized at least a dozen times for psychiatric problems during my youth. I had pursued destructive relationships, along with drugs and alcohol to numb the pain, but they only exacerbated my emotional trauma. My low self-esteem compelled me to seek money and success in order to feel worthwhile, because inside I felt used and worthless.

In my desperate search for happiness, I had gone too far. After the abortion, I realized that I was responsible for the death of my own child, and this secret was making me sick. I wanted desperately to be loved, and to have a new beginning. But there seemed to be no way for a new beginning. I was losing all hope, and I no longer desired to live.

While in the hospital, the combination of depression and years of drug and alcohol addiction caused my immune system to begin to fail. This forced doctors and nurses to wear gloves to touch me, and visitors were required to dress in sterile gowns. The physical pain in my head and neck became so intense that I could barely lift my head off the hospital bed. I felt I would vomit if I moved.

Sunlight caused me to wince, so the blinds had to be shut all the time. My eyes lost the ability to distinguish colors and my world literally appeared to be black and white. I sensed that I was slowly dying.

For two months, the pastor from Barb's church (see Chapter 2) visited me every morning before the sun came up. He would stand bedside my hospital bed and encourage me that it was Christ's desire that I get well. I knew about God, but I didn't have a personal relationship with Jesus at the time.

The pastor acted as if God would forgive everything I'd ever done. He assured me that the Lord could give me a second chance. This seemed too good to be true. The pastor said that God could heal the painful memories from the abuse I'd suffered as a child. I didn't have the courage to tell him about the abortion though; I somehow knew that was something I must never speak about. In my heart, that sin seemed too ugly, too despicable, and too unforgivable.

My **First** (and most important) **Step** toward healing came when I gave my life to Jesus Christ while sitting on my hospital bed in that psychiatric ward. I prayed a disjointed prayer telling God that I was His. But I didn't think there would be much left of my life, since I was so desperately ill. I knew I needed God's forgiveness. I believed enough of what the pastor said to think there still might be a place for me in Heaven.

Right after I accepted Christ, I glanced down at the beautiful engagement ring that I wore. My fiancée was angry that I had a breakdown; and he refused to come to see me. I had been in the hospital for over a week and felt abandoned. The doctor in charge of my case had told me that in order to get well, I needed to end my destructive relationship. The large diamond that was supposed to represent love and protection only reminded me of how very alone I was.

At that moment, the reflective sunlight shining through the hospital window caught the diamond just right. Exquisite rays of multi-colored light seemed to burst from the stone. I thought it was a sign from God that everything would be all right, because within minutes, my fiancée walked in with beautiful yellow roses and asked for my forgiveness. My fiancée's return seemed like an answered prayer, when in actuality it was Satan's deceptive trick to destroy my newly found faith. I didn't realize then that Satan is a real enemy, who is also the king of the counterfeit.

My five-year-old son also came to visit me on the psychiatric ward. He had been my reason to live, and I suppose he was a big part of why I reached out to God. He was a great gift to me, the only good thing that my life had produced. I knew that only God could create someone as precious as Zachary.

After eight weeks, I went home from the hospital and began to study the Bible. My mind was still tormented, and the lithium and other psychiatric drugs clouded my thoughts. The medicine seemed to make me lose any motivation to accomplish even daily tasks.

A few months later in 1987, I tried to return to my job, but I could no longer perform my duties. The breakdown had been complete. It had left me visibly altered. I was no longer a vibrant and motivated corporate representative seeking after the things of the world. Instead, I was a broken woman who desperately wanted to know the God that healed. I had accepted Jesus as my Lord and Savior in the hospital, but I had little knowledge of the Scriptures. Like a nomad, I wandered from church to church searching for answers.

With my conversion came the knowledge that sex before marriage was wrong. Since my fiancée and I had been living together, we married to sanction our sinful lifestyle. In addition to my changed values was the renewed desire for the American dream of a family and a little house with a white picket fence. My husband didn't really want to marry me, but I had given him an ultimatum, "Marry me, or I'll leave."

In retrospect, it would have been wiser to leave, as marriage didn't solve our problems. My attractive and successful husband was a car dealer with an eye for other women. Sometimes he didn't come home at night. The first few months of my marriage I would often cry and regret the years of my sin. I somehow wondered if the life I now lived was the inevitable result of sowing and reaping.

I had grown up in a denomination that had taught me only too well the judgment and wrath of God, but I knew little of His mercy and love. I spent my teen years angry with God for allowing the abuse I had suffered. Then I spent young adulthood in outright rebellion. I felt God hadn't protected me when I was a little girl; therefore I rebelled by breaking every law of His that I could.

My abortion had been the ultimate rebellion. With my conversion came a desire to keep God's laws, but unfortunately my marital situation seemed hopeless. While my marriage was failing, my relationship with Christ was growing stronger. The Holy Spirit began to teach me a revelation of His mercy.

Even though I had lived for years in sin and felt tarnished and used, and incapable of deserving anything good, God kept blessing me. He blessed me with pastors who loved me, and friends who walked through my valleys with me. Sometimes, in a beautiful sunset, or a vibrant rainbow, I could almost feel my gracious Redeemer smiling down on me.

He wanted to give back the things the enemy (Satan) had taken. I began to understand that it grieved God terribly that I had been hurt so much.

I started to think that a baby might be a possibility. I hoped that a baby could help to heal our troubled marriage. It would also be an atonement for my abortion. The desire to conceive became an overwhelming need once again. I had previously promised myself never to discuss having children with my husband. I could not forget our terrible fight while dating caused by my desire to have his baby. Neither of us ever mentioned this incident, but I recalled his accusatory tone and stinging indictment that I was a "murderer." I needed courage to confront this issue because I was losing my husband, and in some ways I felt I was losing my mind. My body actually ached to hold another child.

I waited for what I thought was the right moment, and then I approached my mate about my need. He let me know that this was not a topic for discussion that it had been addressed years earlier, and the answer was still "No."

Later that night, I remember standing in my bedroom grieving because there would be no more children. Despite my sadness, I tried to count my blessings. My son was an adventurous seven-year-old, and I had God on my side. I refused to despair, yet I wondered what would become of our marriage? Without faithfulness or children, what would hold us together?

The answer came sooner than I hoped. My husband's lifestyle began to take its toll. One April evening, he didn't come home for supper. About 10 p.m., I went to the car lot to check on him.

When I walked in, a few of his mechanics were working late in the back. I asked where he was. A couple of them started snickering. I glanced at my brother-in-law who worked at the dealership and said, "What's going on?"

He looked at me sadly, and said, "You'll have to see for yourself." I found my husband in the dark in his office with a beautiful young blonde woman. I ran from the building and got into my car blindly pulling into four lanes of oncoming traffic. It is a miracle I wasn't killed.

I drove home and waited for him to come in with some kind of explanation. He always had an explanation for everything. I waited all night, but he didn't come home. Finally, three days later he returned.

By then I had decided I couldn't live this way anymore. I had become suicidal the last few days, but God had helped me through it.

My husband said he had been thinking about divorcing me but had decided not to. He had driven to Canada to clear his thoughts.

In anger I said, "You don't have to worry about divorcing me, I'm divorcing you."

He walked over picked up my Bible and put it on my lap, and said manipulatively, "Now honey, remember your Christianity, remember forgiveness."

He was trying to use my Christianity against me since there was only one of us living for God. Although I didn't want to leave him, I knew I was becoming a victim once more. That day I filed for a legal separation, and he moved out.

Since my conversion, I had been attending a friend's church, but I needed to find a church where they understood the kinds of problems I was facing. I had learned enough of God's Word to realize that this was a spiritual battle, one that would not be won by natural weapons.

"The weapons we fight with are not the weapons of the world. On the contrary, they have divine power to demolish strongholds. We demolish arguments and every pretension that sets itself up against the knowledge of God, and we take captive every thought to make it obedient to Christ." (II Corinthians 10:4 & 5 NIV)

I was still deeply in love with my husband, or perhaps deeply addicted. I didn't know how I was going to be able to live without him, but I felt that God wanted to renew my mind. In one of my substance abuse meetings I had learned that people could become addicted to people, places, or things. He had been my god, but now, my god had fallen from his pedestal. My love had been a form of idolatry, too. In the past, I often put my love for him over obedience to God.

God faithfully led me to a spirit-filled Bible church with pastors who made me feel safe. I shared about my early life, the abuse, the addiction that I was still fighting, and my obsessive and destructive love for my husband. I don't remember ever sharing the abortion with my new pastors.

I kept praying for God to save my husband and restore our relationship. Tom Ahl, a Christian man who was also a car dealer, tried to counsel us regarding our marriage. In the days to come, Tom would be another link in the chain that God used to heal me of the guilt of my abortion.

Despite Tom's hectic schedule running a large and successful dealership in rural Ohio, he often spends time helping others. When my husband and I were still separated, we met with Tom at his dealership for counsel concerning our marriage. I told Tom that there had been drugs and alcohol in our home. I wanted to live as a Christian, but the daily temptation would always cause me to fall back. During one meeting, I also confronted my spouse about his weakness for other women.

This angered my husband, who said defensively, "She killed her baby." I was shocked and humiliated that he divulged my shameful secret.

Tom never batted an eye, and said firmly, "God forgives her." In this brief statement there was the revelation that God had truly forgiven me. It was like Betty who had visited me and told me that she too had an abortion. I knew God could forgive Betty, but Tom said God had forgiven me, too.

During this time I opened a thrift store to provide for the needs of my son and myself. The store was not just a source of income for us, but it was really a ministry to the hurting. My husband had been my entire life, but now I sensed God encouraging me to take my eyes off my problems, and to focus on helping others. Before my conversion, psychiatrists had taught me to look inside for my answers. Now, God was showing me that through the pain of my broken heart I could be a vessel used for Him. My little boy was in second grade and by having a small business I was able to spend more time with him. We lived in an apartment behind the store and we spent lots of time together going to auctions and stocking shelves to create the new venture. God was helping us to start a new life, and my son seemed relieved with this new stability.

I was 34 years old and I had to accept that my marriage was ending. This was the second time my dream of a family was disintegrating. I realized that without a miracle of God, more children would probably not be a reality.

A year earlier while I was visiting a church in Columbus, Ohio, a very unusual thing happened. A lady I was not acquainted with was seated in the pew in front of me. She had a beautiful little girl with her. I couldn't tell if it was her daughter or granddaughter. There was something very special about this little girl. We kept making eye contact and giggling and smiling at one another.

At the end of the service the woman turned around and said, "God is going to give you the little girl that you have always wanted." Then she told me how she had yearned for a daughter's love and God blessed her with a little girl. She said her daughter was a Christmas Day baby and she had named her Noel. I wondered how this woman had known that I had desperately wanted a baby girl.

I loved my son with my whole heart, but I always felt that the baby I aborted was a girl. Nor could I think about the baby I had miscarried. My children were gone, and I felt that it was my fault. This middle-aged mother's words gave me hope, because she didn't know me. She couldn't know my desire for a little girl unless the Lord had told her. In my heart I clung to the promise, not understanding how God would fulfill it, since my marriage was ending.

In the midst of the grief I was feeling, God gave me another promise. During the praise and worship service at church sometime later, I heard the voice of the Holy Spirit. At the time, I was still seeking to discern my inner voice from God's voice. This day, however, His reply was unmistakable as I agonized over not having more children. I was also struggling with the feeling that I did not belong in church, since I felt so tarnished and worthless.

The Holy Spirit said, "I have given you all the churches, and all the children."

With these words God changed my heart, and began to teach me the **Second Step** of healing, which is the promise of restoration. God always restores, but He does not always do it the way we think He should. With this word, He birthed a supernatural love within my heart for the body of Christ. I'm sorry to say that before this incident, I had been a "spiritual elitist." Subconsciously, I thought the church I attended was the most spiritual of all denominations. I also rarely noticed other people's children. To spare myself emotional pain, I had cut myself off from them due to the guilt I experienced following the abortion.

A few months later, my heart opened miraculously when I encountered a sixteen-year-old girl named Stacey. She was a teenager at a crossroad in her life. We met on the steps of an antique store that was closed. I approached the store and saw Stacey sitting there. She looked like a little angel with her long dark hair framing her beautiful face, but there was something so sad and lost within her eyes. I felt a mother's love for her from the first moment we met.

I invited her to church with me that night. At first I struggled with accepting Stacey into our lives. I had wanted a child of my own. Stacey had a mother who loved her very much, but her father had died before she was born. Stacey's mom worked feverishly to support the four young children that had been left in her charge. Her mom was grateful that I spent time with her, because Stacey was becoming a rebellious teenager. Stacey's love won me over quickly, and she became like my own child. She filled the ache in my heart for a daughter's love.

Stacey began to work in my thrift store and regularly attend church with Zach and me. She had a place at our table, and a special place in my heart. She found healing for her rebellion in a personal relationship with Christ. Although she had made Jesus her Savior before, she now allowed Him to be the Lord of her life. For the next two years God blessed me with a supernatural relationship with this young woman. Since both of us were relatively new converts, we grew in God's ways together.

It would have been easy to say, "No, Lord, I want it my way. I don't want to raise an almost grown child who belongs to someone else." I had to make a choice to accept the daughter the Lord had given me. I consciously commanded my emotions to come under the authority of God's will and to recognize His blessing.

Isaiah says, **"For my thoughts are not your thoughts, neither are your ways my ways," declares the Lord. "As the heavens are higher than the earth, so are my ways higher than your ways and my thoughts than your thoughts." (Isaiah 55:8 & 9 NIV)**

This is the same prophet who told us a chapter earlier that God could give children to the unmarried woman. **"Sing, O barren woman, you who never bore a child, burst into song, shout for joy, you who were never in labor: because more are the children of the desolate woman than of her who has a husband," says the Lord. (Isaiah: 54:1 NIV)**

I needed Stacey's love as much as she needed my guidance. Isaiah said to "shout for joy," that is exactly what Stacey brought into my life, joy. With Stacey's love came my ability to begin to believe that Jesus is truly the Lord of restoration. I knew the process of restoration was only beginning. In order to go through the emotional pain required to achieve wholeness, I had to believe that God would one day totally restore.

The day my divorce was finalized, Stacey bought me a tiny bouquet of flowers. She had been my spiritual daughter for almost a year by then. Her love eased the pain of my failed marriage. She was the first spiritual child that God sent me. In time, there would be others.

CHAPTER FOUR

THE LIE/THE TRUTH

After God blessed me with the vision to open a thrift store, I buried myself in my work. I took care of Zachary, who was now a third grader and spent my spare time with my spiritual daughter, Stacey. I also did volunteer work for my church, and began to attend Bible College.

It had been six years since my abortion. I didn't realize the full impact of what I had done until one night at church when a visiting evangelist showed a movie about abortion. The film displayed a three-month-old fetus that would have become a perfect little human being. When I saw the video of the tiny baby similar to the one I had aborted, I bolted from the sanctuary. Inside I felt that everyone must know the horrible sin I had committed.

The minister didn't say anything about the fact that there were women there who had aborted babies. He didn't share that God still loved them and could not only forgive them, but could also heal them. My guilt felt like a time bomb. I desperately wanted to believe that God might be able to forgive what I had done, but what if people in the church knew? I didn't think they would be as forgiving as God. I didn't realize until much later, that often when misinformed preachers stand in the pulpit denouncing selfish women who have aborted babies, they are speaking to quite a few in their own pews.

About four years after this incident, I heard Dr. Mark Chirona minister at a prophetic conference in Toledo, Ohio. It was February 1993 and a crowd of almost a thousand faithful servants had braved the bitter cold weather to attend the event.

As he ministered, Dr. Chirona said that "Jesus is waiting at the back door of the abortion clinic" to help those who had made this terrible decision. There was almost a frightening kind of silence in the audience, as few understand the Jesus who wants to heal, and forgive us immediately when we sin. I couldn't clap or say, "Amen" when Dr. Chirona spoke, as it would have been an open admission of guilt.

The guilt from my abortion affected my prayer life, too. It was difficult for me to see God as a loving father, because I had not known much love in my life. When I would **"come boldly to throne of grace, to obtain mercy, and find grace to help in time of need,"** (**Hebrews 4:16 KJV** paraphrase) I didn't think I was worthy of God's help. As I would pray and try to be intimate with God, sometimes my horrible sin would rear its ugly head. I would weep in anguish crying out, "God, please forgive me." Even though Christ had hung on the Cross at Calvary to pay for every sin I had committed, I just could not accept that the sin of my abortion was totally gone.

Two things happened about this time that helped me to understand God's forgiveness. Even though I had not realized the call on my life, God's spirit was drawing me. I had a great love for people, although I was somewhat intimidated by the elderly. My grandma could be pretty cantankerous and even though I loved her dearly, her erratic behavior sometimes frightened me. I assumed all older people possessed this same inconsistency.

One day, a lady came into my thrift store and we began discussing ministry. Because of my fear, I jokingly said, "God, will never call me to work with senior citizens." You never say, "never" to God.

The next Sunday in church the people who regularly ministered at the nursing home were in need of help. They couldn't go that afternoon, and so as not to disappoint the old folks they asked for volunteers to minister. I sat there, knowing God would never use me because of my fear. At the same time I felt the tug of the Holy Spirit upon my heart.

I nervously waited for someone to respond to the pastor's plea, but no one did. His voice began to sound almost desperate- and without meaning to my hand seemed to shoot up into the air. He looked relieved as he said, "Great, Christina's willing to go." At that exact moment a woman I did not know said that she and her husband would go along and "show me the ropes."

Jim and Abby were perfectly matched. She was a bubbly middle-aged woman with great spiritual depth. While, he was a somewhat introverted, but always agreeable husband.

We met outside the nursing home later that afternoon. As we stood in the parking lot, for some reason, almost immediately, Abby began to discuss abortion. Inwardly I shivered not from the cold, but from the judgment I knew was about to come. Instead this beautiful silver-haired lady started talking about all the babies who were aborted and how Jesus was taking care of them.

For the first time I did not see a baby ripped apart limb by limb. I mentally visualized infants in soft blankets being cared for by a loving savior. I didn't let Abby know that I had aborted a baby. I quickly changed the subject and acted like we should hurry inside to minister. But as we walked through the entrance of the nursing home, hope exploded within me. My baby was alive in heaven with Jesus! Would it be possible for that child to really forgive me for what I'd done?

An evangelist who visited my church answered that question sooner than I expected. He spoke about a supernatural experience, in which he said he was literally transported to Heaven. He was able to walk and talk with Jesus. This might be difficult for some to believe, but God truly works in miraculous ways. As Jesus and this brother walked in Heaven they reached a place filled with little children. The preacher asked Jesus whose children they were. Jesus explained they were babies that had been aborted. The brother asked Jesus if they were angry at their mothers.

Jesus said, "Oh no, they forgive them. They are waiting for them."

Jesus was taking care of my little one who had forgiven me and was just as anxious to meet me, as I was to meet her.

But how did I know it was a little girl?

My baby's gender and name came in a very unusual way during my prayer time. As I said earlier, I would cry out and ask God over and over for His forgiveness. One day after years of this behavior, God replied in that still small voice from within, "I don't even know what you are talking about." God had spoken this same thing to my pastor concerning the sin he had committed prior to establishing a personal relationship with Christ.

God's Word says, **"Their sins and iniquities will I remember no more."** (Hebrews 10:17 KJV)

The Holy Spirit was trying to tell me that God could no longer remember my sin as I had repented and it was covered by Christ's blood at Calvary. I felt God wanted me to let go of my guilt **"as far as the east is from the west, so far hath he removed our transgressions from us."** (Psalm 103:12 KJV)

In the Old Testament the word transgressions comes from the Hebrew word **pesha** which means rebellion, sin, transgression, or trespass.(1) The denomination I grew up in incorrectly taught me to categorize and qualify sin. I understood that God could forgive my pastor's sin, but pastor hadn't taken another human being's life.

I had to remind myself that sin is sin according to God's law and there is nothing unforgivable except for blasphemy of the Holy Spirit. I wasn't concerned that I had blasphemed the Holy Spirit. I knew that when actual blasphemy occurs, the heart is hardened and unrepentant and blatantly unconcerned about respecting the Holy Spirit.

God used Saul, better known as the Apostle Paul, to illustrate his unconditional forgiveness to me. My pastor didn't need to be forgiven for murder, but Paul did. The Bible says that prior to his Damascus Road conversion he was instrumental in persecuting Christians. Paul even possessed some responsibility for the death of the first martyr for Christ, Stephen.

"On that day a great persecution broke out against the Church at Jerusalem, and all except the apostles were scattered throughout Judea and Samaria. Godly men buried Stephen and mourned deeply for him. But Saul began to destroy the Church. Going from house to house, he dragged off men and women and put them in prison." (Acts 8:1-3 NIV)

Why was Stephen killed? After all, the Bible describes him as a man **"full of faith and power, who did great wonders and miracles among the people."** (Acts 6:8 KJV) He was martyred simply for his stand for the living Christ. (Read Acts Chapter 7)

The King James Version of the Bible further asserts Paul's guilt, **"And Saul was consenting unto his (Stephen's) death."** (Acts 8:1 KJV) As Stephen was being stoned for his belief in Jesus, the Bible records Stephen as saying, **"Behold, I see the heavens opened, and the Son of man standing on the right hand of God."** (Acts 7:56 KJV) ... **"And they stoned Stephen, calling upon God and saying, Lord Jesus, receive my spirit. And he kneeled down, and cried with a loud voice, "Lord, lay not this sin to their charge. And when he had said this, he fell asleep."** (Acts 7:59 & 60 KJV)

Even as he was dying, Stephen was asking God to forgive those who were responsible for his death. After Saul's conversion to Christ, it is understandable that he must have had great guilt concerning his part in Stephen's death and the persecution of so many other believers.

Paul could not have fulfilled the purpose of God for his life shackled with the guilt of his past. That is why Paul so aptly wrote, **"...Forgetting those things which are behind, and reaching forth unto those things which are before. I press toward the prize of the high calling of God in Christ Jesus."** (Philippians 3:13 KJV)

Even as my baby was being ripped from my womb perhaps she was praying that God would forgive me, and all of my well-meaning accomplices of our sin. The **Third Step** of my healing came when I realized that my baby girl was alive in Heaven with Jesus, and that she had forgiven me.

Let's go back to the original question. How do I know I have a little girl named Cassie who is very much alive? It's quite simple, I saw her once. You can call it a vision, or a dream. But whatever you call it, it was real and she's a beautiful baby.

As I was kneeling by my son's bed praying, I was thinking of my aborted child. I had read that it is healing to pray for God to reveal the sex of your baby and to give the baby a name.

As I prayed, I saw Jesus standing with a baby in his arms. The baby was wrapped tightly in a soft pink blanket. He was holding her so lovingly. Then I saw myself approach Jesus knowing that He was holding my baby. I knew from the color of the blanket that she was a little girl. Inside I had always known that. Instinctively, I knew her name, too.

The next moment I was holding her in my arms. She had a beautiful little face with big blue eyes and chubby little cheeks. Cassie. Cassandra, it really was her. I couldn't believe it. I thought I would live with the torment of never holding my baby, but here she was resting safely in my arms!

I couldn't believe that she wasn't deformed. I knew what I had done to her. After all those years of the nightmares of her being ripped apart, I had to see for myself. I pulled the plush blanket back and looked at her little hands. They were perfect; all her fingers were there. The same thing with her feet; her toes were perfect, too. In that instant a tremendous flow of God's healing power surged through my body. My Cassie was whole. Jesus had taken wonderful care of her.

Then Jesus motioned for me to give Cassie back to Him. He didn't speak, but I knew that she must go with Him and that I must complete the work that He had called me to do here. I kissed her chubby cheek, and handed Cassie back to Jesus.

The pain of returning her after finally seeing her would have been too much to bear, but Jesus reached out and put His hand on my heart and my forehead. He comforted me with His love, a love that is able to heal the broken heart and restore damaged emotions.

The day was Nov. 1, 1994, almost 11 years since my abortion. I wept when the vision disappeared. I knew that I would probably not see my daughter again upon this Earth. Yet, God had destroyed the lie that the enemy of my soul had condemned me with by convincing me that I committed the unpardonable sin. Seeing my baby in that vision, I realized the truth, that she was very much alive and that both Jesus and Cassie had forgiven me. I knew that I had to somehow make her life mean something, so that her death was not in vain.

All the terrible grief I had experienced could be used as a tool in the Holy Spirit's hand to prevent others from making this tragic mistake. God could also use my pain to help heal those who had been as ignorant as I once had been concerning abortion.

The Holy Spirit blessed me as I ended my prayer time that day with a poem from my daughter. Although I've never heard her voice, the still small voice of God spoke from within the words that I desperately needed to hear:

Cassie's Prayer
Don't grieve for me anymore, Mama
I'm so happy here
I want you to be happy, too
I know that you didn't understand
that I was a life
A person created to give love
Please receive my love now
as well as my forgiveness
Know I'm waiting for you
Mama, Jesus loves you
He's taking good care of me
Please don't be sad anymore
We'll be together soon

Love, Cassie

CHAPTER FIVE

THE LAUNDROMAT

I was still kneeling in God's presence, thanking Him for allowing me a healing vision of my Cassie, when a knock at the back door brought me back to reality. I felt disoriented and somewhat irritated at the interruption, but there was a sound of urgency about this knock.

I walked to the door, but before opening it, I drew the curtain back and looked out the window. Judith, one of my spiritual daughters, was standing on the steps looking very distraught. Hurriedly, I unlocked the door and ushered her in. Judy sat down at my kitchen table and began to pour out her heart to me. She had sinned years earlier and was unable to bear the secret anymore. Judy blurted out the details of the sad story, which I had never heard before. Then she waited for me to reply.

She was in terrible pain and had carried around an incredible amount of guilt for years. In that moment I understood Judy so much better. I saw the trap Satan had devised to hold her in sin-consciousness. She had committed a terrible sin, and I could see that she thought it was her "unpardonable" sin, just like my abortion was for me.

I groped for words to help her. Judy had never seen me at a loss for words, and interpreted my silence and stammering as a sign that she really had messed up more than God's grace could handle.

Her situation was so devastating that I was struggling within myself to find an answer for her. I prayed silently, "Oh, God, how do I help her?"

I sensed the Lord saying, "Tell her about your abortion."

I couldn't believe that was God. I thought I must be confused as I was just reentering reality after a supernatural encounter concerning my vision of Jesus with Cassie. Besides, I never talked about the abortion. I couldn't. I thought it would destroy me to even speak of it.

The still small voice came again. "Tell her about the abortion." I looked at Judy's distressed face. Due to my long silence, she was becoming desperate and looked like a cornered animal that was about to bolt.

I had to try to comfort her. So, even though it didn't make any sense to me, I said, "Judy, I need to tell you about something that happened to me a long time ago."

I explained how I thought I had miscarried a baby in my early twenties, because of a failed suicide attempt. Even in the midst of her pain, she looked sympathetic. Then I continued on and said, "Actually, I have two babies in heaven." I explained that when my son was three-years-old, I was a financially and emotionally struggling single mom who had become pregnant again. I told her the sordid details of my life back then and how I chose abortion to end the life of my baby.

I explained the phenomenon of "anniversary depression." How for the first few years the anniversary of my baby's death passed without notice, or at least without remembrance of great emotional pain specifically on the date of my abortion. At the time, there was so much pain and denial about everything on a day-to-day basis.

Since she knew little about my past, I briefly recounted the details of my drug use at the time of my abortion. I described my climb up the corporate ladder, which hadn't included another child, and the destructive relationships, which left me alone and condemned.

There was one thing in my life that was good, my little boy, who was growing up rapidly. He didn't realize what a mess his mother was. He simply loved me unconditionally. Judy knew that thirteen-year-old Zach was my life. She nodded politely at my sad tale, probably wondering what it had to do with her sin.

Judith had not known me in the days when my son was born in a shelter, and my only source of income was a meager welfare check. She knew me as the owner of a successful thrift and antique store who ministered to hurting people. She didn't realize that I had learned how to operate a thrift store when I could only afford to buy our clothes and possessions at thrift stores. When Zachary was small even his shoes had first belonged to someone else's child.

I explained to her that I hadn't seen the glob of tissue inside of me as a baby. I saw it as something that threatened my son's and my existence — something that I could not emotionally handle. Something I must get rid of, just like other women before me, who went to back alley abortionists.

After I gave my life to Christ, I realized how cruel and selfish I'd been. But it was the Devil, who had deceived me, and millions of women like me. After all, **John 10:10** says, **"The thief cometh not, but for to steal, kill and destroy..." KJV**

My baby was a gift from God. Just because she was conceived in sin, made her no less of a gift. If the baby was not a gift to me, she could have been a gift for someone else. But in my self-deception, I destroyed the beautiful gift God had given me. I looked at Judith and said, "What sin could be worse than murdering your own child?"

I told her the anniversary of my abortion was once again approaching. I explained that since I had become a Christian and understood the horrible thing I had done, the grief was sometimes worse. I didn't have the drugs and alcohol to numb the pain. When I looked at my wonderful son who was now a teenager, I felt such grief wondering what my other child would have been like.

I realized too late that there were all kinds of options. A childless family would have been eternally grateful to raise my baby. Or God could have even helped me to put an extra plate on the table, and buy two pairs of shoes at the thrift store.

Yes, I was selfish. When we don't know Jesus we must survive by the labor of our own hands. It is an overwhelming task! Even when we do know Him, often our intellectual mind will tell us there is no way out. But that is all the enemy's deception. As I explained the traumatizing aftermath of my abortion, Judy looked shocked.

Had my sin horrified her, as I had feared? I knew I shouldn't have spoken of it. I felt naked and ashamed. Why had I betrayed my secret?

But she began to speak and to minister to me. She was saddened that she had known me for so long, and had not known about the pain of losing my babies. She seemed to understand instantly why she was so important to me.

Then suddenly it hit me. God is so wise. Not only is sin, sin. But guilt is guilt. Our sins were different but the effect was the same — a guilt that was more than we could bear. I shared my vision of a few moments earlier. I knew God was beginning to heal me, but I was going to have to allow it.

I told her that she was also going to have to accept God's forgiveness by faith and go on. There was nothing either one of us could do to change our past, but we could change the future by becoming all that God intended for us to be. As I was speaking to her about the need for her to receive God's forgiveness, I was ministering to myself.

We both began praying for each other that God would heal us. He was our only hope. In just a few weeks it would once again be Dec. 3, the anniversary of my abortion. Usually as the date neared I would descend into a deep pit of depression. Some years I feared that I wouldn't make it back out.

But this year I had my vision, and the relief of sharing my terrible secret with someone. Someone, who would be praying for me. Jumping ahead to **Step 7** — healing any past trauma finds its origin in sharing our sin with a non-judgmental party, and with those we've wronged. (We will discuss this step in greater detail in Chapter 8) **James 5:16 KJV** says, **"Confess your faults one to another, and pray one for another, that ye may be healed. The effectual fervent prayer of a righteous man availeth much."**

Judith's prayers were to be answered sooner than I anticipated as my anniversary date brought one more link in God's healing chain.

When I awoke on Dec. 3, it was cold and dreary, much like all the preceding years. I always fight depression by keeping myself busy, so I decided I would go to the Laundromat and try to do something productive, since my store was closed that day.

My heart was heavy and I felt terribly alone. My little boy was now a teenager in junior high. He was at school and the day loomed

ahead of me like a dreaded enemy. I gathered our clothes and headed
to the Laundromat.

If you are willing to listen, people will often tell you their
problems as they do their laundry. I was not only willing but I
shared Jesus with them, as He is the answer to every problem we
have.

Once I was even blessed to lead a troubled young man to the
Lord, right at the Laundromat. Normally I looked at doing the
wash as an evangelistic outing, but this day I dreaded even being
awake.

I loaded the washer, grabbed a cup of bitter instant coffee and
reached for a magazine from the stack on the counter. I picked a
Guidepost as they had ministered to me so much when I had been
a patient on the psychiatric ward years earlier. God knew I needed
to be ministered to that day.

I started to read a story about a couple named Terry and Anne
Sternard and their five-year-old son T.J. The Sternards also had an
eight-year-old daughter, Samantha, who was learning to ride horses.
The family had gone on an outing to a horse stable on the outskirts
of Denver. As Samantha was riding, T.J. wandered off to a frozen
creek near the stables and fell into the icy water. By the time they
found him, he had been in the water a long time. They rushed T.J.
to the hospital where doctors were able to find a heartbeat, but a
short time later the little boy died.

T.J. had been so excited about Christmas approaching. He told
his mom he had a special present that he was saving for her. He
showed her the little box several times. After T.J. died his Mom
thought of the little gift that had been so important to him. She
went to the closet and found the box, which should have been
opened on Christmas.

According to the article, neither Anne nor her husband had a
close relationship with Jesus. She was desperately in need of comfort, and answers to questions that tragedy brings. She had hoped
to find some kind of answer inside the box. When she opened the
present, she found a little gold cross on a chain. It was like her son
knew that he wouldn't be there for Christmas, but that he'd left a

sign that he had gone to his new home in Heaven, and that the only way there was the way of the Cross.

He'd left another sign — one for me. As I read the touching story, my eyes began to blur with tears. I thought my blurred vision must have caused me to misread the date when this tragic event had occurred. I looked again. T.J. had gone home to be with Jesus at almost the same moment Cassie had left this earth on the afternoon of Dec. 3, 1983.(1)

My baby died tragically in an Akron abortion clinic the very afternoon that an icy pond had caused the Sternards to lose their son. It gave me comfort that our children had entered Heaven at the same time.

I don't know what the other Laundromat patrons thought as I stood there holding a *Guidepost* magazine with tears streaming down my face, but I didn't care. God was reaching out to comfort me, by showing me that others had suffered this pain. **"Who comforts us in all our troubles, so that we can comfort those in any trouble with the comfort we ourselves have received from God." (2 Cor. 1:4 NIV)**

As I read on I found that the death of their precious son had led them to the feet of our loving Savior. Just as Cassie's death had led me to find forgiveness and acceptance at the same Cross.

What Satan had intended for evil **"God intended it for good to accomplish what is now being done, the saving of many lives." (Genesis 50:20 NIV)**

My life may not have been saved that day, but God definitely further let me experience His healing virtue. I went home and wrote this couple, sharing how much their testimony had meant to me. I believe I told them that I realized I did not have the right to grieve as they did, but that I grieved nonetheless.

A few weeks later I received a beautiful letter from T.J.'s mom, Anne Sternad. Anne explained her belief about the power of Christ's forgiveness. The envelope contained a gift that meant more to me than words could ever express. Tucked inside was a small pastel pink booklet containing helpful information for those who have experienced the death of a child.

This was the first time that any other person on this earth had acknowledged that my daughter was a real human being, and that her death was a terrible loss. Somehow, by including the booklet that dear mother had given me permission to grieve. **Step 4** of my healing came in giving myself permission to grieve.

There is so much self-persecution following abortion that it often takes another individual to establish the victim's right to grieve. This is why **Step 7** (sharing our sin with a non-judgmental party or with those we've wronged) and **Step 4** are often closely intertwined.

CHAPTER SIX

FORGIVEN

Finding Peace through Forgiveness

According to the Alan Guttmacher Institute, "Nearly half of all American women will have had at least one abortion by age 45."(1) This seems like an alarmingly high statistic, but remember millions of babies have been aborted. Yet, few women in society seem to speak openly about having had an abortion.

Where are these post-abortive women? They are sitting next to you in church, checking out your groceries at the supermarket, taking your blood pressure at the doctor's office, or living with you in your own house. In other words, these women are everywhere. They need the love and healing power that Jesus offers – and Jesus most often works through His people to display His healing touch.

One person that God used to help me heal was my own son, Zachary. Because I was a single mom and we spent a great deal of time together, Zach and I became extremely close. It was explained in detail in Chapter 3, that when my son was five years old, I was hospitalized for several months on a psychiatric ward. The childhood abuse I had experienced, and the sinful life that ensued, formed the catalyst for a nervous breakdown.

God allowed the breakdown to occur, so that I could look up to find Jesus Christ, but things did not change instantly for me. As a young Christian, I tried to hide my emotional ups and downs from my son, because I knew my instability frightened him.

Zach knew that before he was born, I had nearly died several times from suicide attempts. This was no secret; my family members would also get extremely concerned, since I had been hospitalized many times for depression. If I became depressed and withdrawn, I'd try to mask the pain and put on a "happy face" at least in front of Zachary.

Zach was never really fooled. He had the ability to see past my façade. Year after year, when the anniversary depression connected with my abortion would come, our household changed. Everything joyful turned dark and gloomy. Since Christmas was on the way, I wanted it to be a happy time for him. But no matter how hard I tried, December usually found me in a black hole of despair.

Now Zachary was in junior high. I had always talked to him openly about alcohol, drugs and sexual abuse. I didn't want the enemy to target him for an attack in these areas. From the time he was just a small boy, I warned Zach not to let anyone touch his body in areas that were private. I explained that he should not be afraid, just let me know if an adult threatened him. But I had never talked to him about abortion. How would my son feel about me then? I didn't have to tell Zach about my abortion, God let him find out in a very unusual way.

It was almost a decade ago, on a winter afternoon when I found myself once again engulfed in the grief of my lost child. It seemed even more difficult as I was aging and realized that God was probably not going to give me back a natural child to replace the one I had aborted. For years, I clung to the Scripture in Isaiah, **"The children, which thou shalt have after thou hast lost the other, shall say again in thine ears, The place is too strait for me: give place to me that I may dwell."** (Isaiah 49:20 KJV)

The New International Version of the Bible says it a little differently, **"The children born during your bereavement will yet say in your hearing 'this place is too small for us; give us more space to live in.' Then you will say in your heart, 'Who bore me these? I was bereaved and barren; I was exiled and rejected. Who brought these up? I was left alone, but these — where have they come from?'"** (Isaiah 49:20 & 21 NIV)

It can be difficult for any woman as she ages to realize that she probably won't have more children. It can be especially heartbreaking for those of us who have made the devastating decision to abort, ending our own child's life.

Thinking I was alone in our apartment since Zach was at school, I started sobbing. I hadn't allowed myself to grieve before, but now I felt God gave me His permission.

I lay prostrate on my son's bed — buried my head in his comforter and wept inconsolably, losing track of time. I didn't hear the door open, or my son's footsteps as he approached. The first thing I heard was his frightened question, "Mom, what's wrong? You're crying like you killed somebody."

The wording of his question pierced my pained heart and my honest answer poured out of me, "I did." Zach knows I'm a serious person, who wouldn't joke about something like that. He could tell that what I was saying was true. His horrified look seemed to say, "How, when, why, who?" all at the same time.

Zachary's fear brought me back to reality and I knew it was time to explain the truth to him. It was his sister. He had a right to know.

Some might think he was too young, but I truly believe it was God's timing. December's unexplainable depressions were beginning to affect him, too. Not only that, but he was in his teen years. In the near future Zach was going to need to make some decisions about dating, sex and abortion that every young person must face.

I told him the story without going into detail. Even at his tender age, he seemed to somehow understand why December had been such a rough time at our house. I felt a tremendous relief that I wasn't a hypocrite any longer. I had told my son my deepest darkest secret and like God, he still loved me.

Zachary did ask me if I had thought of aborting him. I could see the hurt in his eyes as he asked me this question. It was so hard to explain how I had once felt abortion was okay, but that the devastating aftermath of my own abortion convinced me to change my belief.

God had forgiven me, my son had forgiven me, even Cassie had forgiven me, but I was still having a tough time forgiving myself. Maybe that's because I hadn't completely forgiven others.

After all, the Bible says, **"Therefore I say unto you, what things you desire, when ye pray, believe that ye receive them, and ye shall have them. And when ye stand praying, forgive, if ye have aught against any: that our Father also which is in heaven may forgive you your trespasses. But if ye do not**

forgive, neither will your Father which is in heaven forgive your trespasses." (Mark 11:24-26 KJV)

Step 5 of my healing involved forgiving others, so that I could receive forgiveness. Over the years I had worked on some really big issues dealing with forgiveness. At the top of the list were: childhood sexual abuse, rejection, abuse by doctors while institutionalized, abandonment while pregnant, and unfaithfulness in marriage. I thought God had helped me to forgive these serious violations that had been part of my young life. Yet, I found myself still forfeiting the grace of God, as there was one man I had steadfastly refused to forgive for almost twenty years. His name was Sam and he had spent the last two decades in prison for killing my high school friend, Ben.

I need to travel back to my Senior Year of High School to explain the story. I spent the majority of that year in a state institution for the mentally ill.

It was difficult for my classmates to be friends with me, as mental illness carried a deadly stigma 30 years ago. Some of my peers were afraid that my tormented state might be contagious. But my friend Ben didn't care what others thought.

When I was released from the state institution, he would pick me up in his little yellow car and take me to the park, out to eat, or to his friends for school parties. He was a senior at another school in our city. His classmates and some of mine ridiculed him for spending time with me. One of them even asked him, "Don't you know that she's crazy?"

Ben told his friends he didn't care what they said, he thought I was a nice girl and enjoyed being with me.

Ben had sandy blond hair and blue eyes. He made me laugh, and in those days I didn't laugh too often. But there was something that seemed to torment Ben, too. After graduation, he slowly started changing. He ran with the wrong crowd and gravitated towards everything that represented life on the edge.

Physically, Ben was a big man, who seemed to get bigger year after year. By the time he was in his early twenties, he had quite a reputation as the town bully. Even some of the local police officers began to fear him, after he ripped a lavatory out of a jail cell with his bare hands. One thing about Ben that didn't change was that he was very protective of me.

One night Ben saved my life. I was in my early twenties, and by then I was really strung out on drugs. It was a few years before my son was born, and I felt I had no reason to live. I was so high that I literally sat in the middle of a busy street waiting for a car to come and run over me and put me out of my misery. It was a snowy night and visibility was almost nonexistent. Ben found me in the street and carried me out of harm's way. Some would say it was luck that he happened by, but I believed God used him to rescue me.

I only wish God could have used me to rescue him. However, I do believe I was called to warn him. One afternoon while we were talking, I told Ben he had to quit bullying people. I said, "If you don't stop stripping people of their pride, someone is going to kill you." That's exactly what happened a few months later.

Ben was in a bar one night when he began fighting with another young man named Sam, who was smaller than Ben. He humiliated and intimidated Sam, who was high on drugs at the time. Sam went home, got a gun, and came back and shot Ben. Ben died instantly. He was in his twenties and left a wife, two children, sisters, brothers, parents and friends. Most of all he left a future that was never to be fulfilled.

I was 25 years old when Ben was killed and expecting my son Zachary. At his funeral service I glanced down at my pregnant belly. It seemed so cruel that a life was growing inside of me, when Ben's life had ended so prematurely. I felt the first seeds of bitterness begin to take root in my heart. I didn't know the Lord then, so I didn't worry about whether people had a personal relationship with Christ when they died. The pastor who ministered at the funeral pulled out a slip of paper found in Ben's boyhood Bible that talked about Jesus.

Where Ben is now is for God to judge, but Sam's fate was decided by the court system decades ago. He's been serving a life sentence for the murder ever since. Over the years, I heard that Sam had become a model prisoner and had turned his life around.

He reportedly warned those in contact with him about the dangers of drugs and alcohol. I had also been told that he had found peace with God.

A close relative of mine kept in contact with Sam. They were friends and roommates before Sam went to prison. Over the years, my relative would often comment about the amazing changes in Sam's life, despite the fact that he was serving a life sentence. I always listened and nodded politely, but inside of me a little voice would say, "That's nice, but Ben's dead."

About a year after I became a TV reporter, I thought I heard the still small voice of God saying that I needed to go into the prison to interview Sam. Part of my job as a producer for a daily testimonial show was doing features on people like Sam, who had changed their lives with God's help. At the time, I was also speaking about once a month in the prison where Sam was incarcerated. Although I had no connection with him, I knew that because of my TV credentials, finding him wouldn't be a problem.

I was procrastinating though, because I couldn't believe that God would possibly want me to go into the prison and interview Sam. Certainly, I thought God would know that would be too difficult for me emotionally. But that nagging little voice inside just wouldn't go away.

After you serve God for a while, you realize that He truly does work in mysterious ways. Often instead of allowing His children to hide from something that has hurt them traumatically, God will actually make them confront it.

Finally, after the conviction wouldn't leave, I obeyed God. I called my family member and asked him to speak to Sam about my desire to do an interview with him. My relative said that Sam had recently gone before the parole board, and after almost 20 years of incarceration for Ben's murder, he was denied parole. He would not see the parole board again for five years. He said Sam was disappointed, but that he realized it was all part of God's plan.

When I heard this, I thought that Sam must have truly achieved a spiritual depth that few Christians ever realize. I've seen Christians walk away from God simply because they weren't "blessed" with the material possession they prayed for, or because in some other way they felt that God failed them.

Here was a man who seemed to truly understand that the will of God for our lives sometimes includes suffering. Because Christ forgives our sin does not negate the consequence that sin often carries. **I Peter 4:19** says, **"So then, those who suffer according to God's will should commit themselves to their faithful Creator and continue to do good." (NIV)**

Those who work in the penal system often have a disdain for inmates who boast about their jailhouse conversions — believing that this will somehow purchase their freedom. This inmate seemed to understand that God was allowing him to stay in prison so that His perfect will could be accomplished.

After weighing the pros and cons of doing a television interview, Sam decided to do it. He thought it might be of benefit to those caught up in the lifestyle he once embraced. He also realized that this kind of exposure could portray him in a negative light. He decided to risk this to help others.

The day before I was scheduled to go into the prison to shoot the interview, I began having second thoughts. I hadn't seen Sam; I had only corresponded with him through others, and some lengthy paperwork that had been necessary for the state to grant the interview. My old bitterness was surfacing.

While waiting in line at the post office, I started having a little argument with God. I know that you never win this kind of dialogue, but sometimes our emotions try to prevail. I asked God very petulantly, "Why are you making me do this? I don't want to interview him. God, he's a murderer."

God replied very firmly, "So are you."

I knew instinctively that God was referring to my abortion.

From a theological sense God's voice momentarily shocked me. After all, I minister to others quite often from **Hebrews 10:17**, where God says, **"Their sins and lawless acts I will remember no more." (NIV)**

I wanted to say out loud, "God, that's not fair, my abortion was atoned for by Jesus' blood. You're the one who told me that yourself." However, I knew enough Scriptural law to realize I had just seen the law of sowing and reaping take effect. If I was going to bring up Sam's sin to God, God had every right to remind me of mine.

The next day, I met Sam. He wasn't at all what I expected. He was a very intelligent man who was extremely honest. As I asked the questions that I had prepared for the interview, Sam's answers came automatically. He was not trying to impress anyone. I had worked in media long enough to discern when that's happening, but he was trying to be accurate.

For about an hour Sam presented the events that had led up to Ben's death including his troubled adolescence plagued by alcohol and drug use. His desire to be a tough guy, but being afraid — afraid that somebody would find out that inside he wasn't really that tough.

The alcohol and drug addiction escalated to the night of June 29, 1980. He was in what he describes as a "rough and tumble kind of bar" where he started to fight with Ben. Ben humiliated him, and Sam's pride couldn't take that. He went home found a gun, came back, and waited outside of the bar. As Ben was leaving Sam emptied the chamber of the gun into Ben's body. Sam said that he didn't even remember pulling the trigger that night, because he was too high on drugs and alcohol. He does remember standing over Ben's collapsed form with the gun in his hand.

Now more than twenty years later, Sam is a convicted murderer serving a life sentence.* He said he hadn't minded being labeled a murderer so much when he was young. It brought a kind of fear to other prisoners, giving him some protection. Although, the stigma of being a murderer really began to bother him as he grew older. "You can't be labeled anything worse," he said candidly.

Sam didn't know how well I understood the heavy burden of being a convicted murderer. I hadn't been convicted by society; they had even sanctioned my murder. Once I came to know Christ's commandments, I knew that I, too, was a murderer. I wanted to tell Sam that I understood, and that we shared the same label. I couldn't, since the warden's assistant stood along the wall guarding our conversation.

I didn't tell Sam that Ben was my friend, either, that would have been too unprofessional. When I asked my questions, I waited for him to blame Ben for being such a bully and provoking the fight. Sam didn't do that; instead he accepted accountability for his crime.

I remembered back to my abortion when I was first pregnant blaming my boyfriend, blaming my failed birth control, even blaming God. However, I finally realized there was no one to blame but myself. Sam's honesty was unwrapping the tentacles of bitterness that had held my heart captive for twenty years. I asked Sam what he would say to Ben's family and friends if he had the opportunity.

He shook his head sadly and said, "I think today of what I altered. The children that were never born, the birthday parties the man will never attend."

He confessed that what he took away that was probably the greatest loss was life itself. "As long as there's life there is hope," he added remorsefully. I was reminded of the Scripture in **Ecclesiastes 9:4, "Anyone who is among the living has hope..." (NIV)**

My thoughts went to Cassie, about the life experiences she, too, would never have. She would never experience the thrill of a first date, or attend a High School prom. There would be no pretty white dress and veil for her wedding day, no opportunity to love or be loved by a man, nor children for her to bear. I had removed the hope of life in a matter of seconds on an abortionist's table. Sam had stolen these same things from Ben and his family and friends. He couldn't change the past, anymore than I could.

Something in me broke at that moment. Somehow, my enemy had become my friend, because we were both murderers. Sam said that it had almost driven him insane trying to deal with the guilt of what he'd done. "How could he pay for his crime?" he asked. With his life, with life in prison, what was the right punishment?

I vividly saw myself in his words. Year after year, I grieved and couldn't be consoled, because I was too ashamed to tell anyone I needed help. I had given myself a life sentence, too, but until I met Sam I didn't have a hope for parole.

God healed something inside of me that day in the prison that far exceeded any bitterness I held towards Sam. God showed me a man who had the courage to tell the whole truth in the hope that it might help others. For the first time, I fully understood God's gift of forgiveness extended to another, and I knew that same gift was available for me, no matter what. Despite the fact he was locked in a prison cell, Sam Cartwright seemed to be a free man.

I wanted to have that freedom, too. However, a few months later it was December again, and somehow I had plunged back into the dark hole of despair. One evening, my son, Zachary, and I were in a restaurant eating. I must have appeared withdrawn and distracted, because Zach looked at me with concern and tentatively asked, "Is it Cassie?"

What a sensitive young man he was becoming. I was so self-absorbed in my painful memories, that I wasn't aware of how my depressions were affecting him. Just hearing Zachary say Cassie's name out loud jarred me back into reality.

I nodded my head sadly. Despite my new revelation of forgiveness, I was still hanging onto the pain. Even though it had been fourteen years, I had never buried my daughter. It was time for her funeral.

Although the above story of Ben and Sam is true, their names have been changed to protect them and their families.

*Sam Cartwright was released from prison in 2001

CHAPTER SEVEN

CASSIE'S FUNERAL

The anniversary depression wasn't the same as other years. This year my paternal grandmother had died and she was going to be buried the same day that my abortion had taken place. This really confused me emotionally, because I hadn't particularly liked my grandmother.

Grandma wasn't a part of my childhood, since she lived on the other side of the country. I had only seen her once in the past 25 years. The one time I had visited with her, I was in California vacationing and decided to look her up. My antagonism stemmed from the fact that she had given my dad away when he was only a toddler. I believed that a lot of the problems that my family experienced probably started when Grandma took off for the coast. When she left she took her daughters with her, but left my father to be raised by elderly relatives.

Through the years when I was growing up, Dad seemed to avoid talking about the fact that Grandma had left him. Once in awhile, he would let a sentence slip that made me realize he was still in pain over the rejection. When I was a child, anytime she wanted to come for a visit, he welcomed her into our home. She didn't seem like a bad woman, just someone I didn't really know who had abandoned my dad.

The one time I did go to see her as an adult, it seemed that she had developed some fantasy past. She told me stories about Dad, and about taking care of him as a child. She wasn't there to take care of him, so I knew that she had created this delusion to appease her guilt. The visit left me empty and deflated and I never saw her alive again.

Now they were shipping her body "home" for burial. When I was growing up, my dad had taught me a very valuable lesson about the dead. Never canonize them, but never disrespect them, either. It was time to bury Grandma and I knew that I must respect the situation.

I thought it would be nice to get a poinsettia, since it was December. When I arrived at the funeral home I needed to check with the funeral director about the flowers. As I stepped into the back room I ran right into my Grandma's coffin. The funeral director looked startled. I began to explain about the flowers, but I could barely take my eyes off the coffin.

Grandma was really dead. This was finally becoming real to me. Later at the visitation, I stood over Grandma's open casket and was shocked at her white hair and finely veined skin. She was so pale that her skin seemed translucent. The little purple veins at her temples were so visible that she looked like a fragile porcelain doll.

I had remembered her as a fiery redhead with a sharp tongue. In the coffin was the body of a feeble old woman who had fought her last life battle, and appeared to be at peace. It didn't matter how she looked, I was angry with her. She had walked away and left my dad when he was too young to understand. I looked down at her and said accusingly, "How could you do that to your own son?" I had forsaken God's mercy once again. The Holy Spirit's gentle voice reminded me that tomorrow would mark fourteen years since I had taken my own child's life. The real question was, "How could I have done that to my daughter?"

The answer to both questions came so rapidly. "Sin." Grandma and I had both been deceived by the enemy, and had made terrible choices that had caused us to lose our children. She was not my enemy, just an old woman who had spent her last days in such emotional pain that she literally believed she had raised a child she had abandoned.

In that instant, I'd finally forgiven her. My decision to forgive her, made it easy to act respectful. In reality, Grandma was just another poor victim in Satan's tangled web. She needed to be buried with dignity; after all, she had wanted to come "home."

The next morning there were only about a dozen people at the funeral. It was Dec. 3, 1997, exactly fourteen years to the day since my abortion.

During the funeral I thought of Cassie. Every song and every Scripture somehow made me think of her. For a moment I even tried to pretend that my daughter was in the coffin, because I knew I needed to bury her. But this was Grandma's funeral, I didn't want to go through life pretending as Grandma had.

My father carried his mother's coffin to the cemetery. He was respectful just as he had taught me, but something about him seemed so terribly sad. He resembled a small child, who understood he was being abandoned forever.

My dad was finally putting his painful past with his mother to rest. You could see the resignation in the way he carried himself that day. He didn't have to try to be accepted by her anymore.

I had to put my relationship with my daughter to rest, too. I couldn't continue to carry this grief for the rest of my life. I felt she needed to have a funeral, but how?

As I was reading the local newspaper, God's answer came. Chiles and Sons-Laman Funeral Home was having its annual Tree of Remembrance Memorial Service that following Saturday. Surely, God didn't want me to bury my child with all those strangers, but I ripped the advertisement out of the newspaper just in case.

Once in awhile, I would pick the ad up and ponder what God might want me to do. I desperately wanted to get well, but I still needed closure. Deep within, I sensed that **Step 6** of my healing included having a ceremony for Cassie, so that I could find peace. I had to be willing to experience the grief in order to receive comfort. That's why the Bible says, **"Blessed are those who mourn, for they will be comforted."** (Matthew 5:4 NIV)

During a death it's often easy to stuff your emotions deep inside yourself and numb yourself to the intense pain of your loss. That's why funeral services are such a wonderful gift to the loved ones left behind. You get to experience the pain of grief amid loving supporters who can encourage you in the midst of your loss.

The Bible also says, **"Rejoice with those who rejoice; mourn with those who mourn."** (Romans 12:15 NIV) I felt I needed to share my loss with others who were also mourning. Although, other people seemed to have more of a right to grieve than I did, since I was responsible for my daughter's death. Yet, through **Step 4** of the healing process, I had accepted that God wanted me to have that right, too. (See Chapter 5)

Cassie had died on the third of December, and the memorial service was scheduled for the sixth of December. Three days was the appropriate time to wait between a death and the interment service.

On Friday evening, a friend from work stopped and asked if I would like to go to a football game the next day. I said, "Thanks, but I have plans for tomorrow." I wasn't sure if I had plans or not, because I didn't know if I had the courage to carry out what I believed the Lord was showing me to do.

He heard the hesitation in my voice concerning my plans. Just then he glanced down at the ad, which was now in clear sight on the cabinet top. He said sympathetically, "Would you like me to go with you?"

My friend was genuinely concerned for me. I had been acting withdrawn all week. I'm sure people thought that my detachment stemmed from the emotion of burying my grandmother.

I told him how much I appreciated his support, but that "I needed to do this alone." I did tell him that I would greatly appreciate his prayers.

The next morning, I wrestled with myself about the need to attend the service. Then by mid-afternoon, an hour before the event was to occur, I found myself reaching for the phone. I dialed the number for the memorial service that was listed in the advertisement.

The ad said that there was to be a large Christmas tree set up in the lobby of the funeral home. Mourners would be given an ornament in memory of his or her loved one. Then there would be a brief service with a few local ministers with refreshments following. The ad also said to call for reservations.

I made the phone call in obedience to what I thought was God's leading. However, I was convinced that because I had not made reservations earlier, it would be impossible for me to attend.

A young man answered the phone, "Chiles and Sons-Laman Funeral Homes, Duane Hinkle speaking."

"Yes, I'm calling about the memorial service that you're having this afternoon. I'm sure it's too late to come?"

The young man had a very kind voice and assured me that it wasn't too late, and that there would be room for me.

"But, I don't have reservations," I argued. Inwardly I was hoping that he would let me off the hook, so I wouldn't have to humble myself and make a public display of my grief.

I knew though that the book of Peter says that, "God opposes the proud but gives grace to the humble." That passage continues, **"Humble yourself therefore, under God's mighty hand, that he may lift you up in due time. Cast all your anxiety on him because he cares for you." (I Peter 5:5-7 NIV)**

I desperately needed God's grace to totally heal my grief. I could not be prideful about my need for God's help. I would have to do it His way, trusting that He would walk with me every step.

Even though he was young, Duane was a very efficient funeral director. Somehow in his heart, he knew I needed to be at that service. He assured me once again that reservations weren't necessary. He took my name and said that they would be expecting me.

God had me hooked. I promised Duane I would be there, and I believe in keeping my word. Before I was a Christian I would not always keep promises that I made. God once showed me that this was a form of lying and that it showed disrespect for the feelings of others. The Bible confirms this by stating that a man who enjoys God's presence in his life, **"...keeps his oath even when it hurts." (Psalm 15:4 NIV)**

In obedience, I began to dress. I threw on my long black skirt and a black sweater that was decorated with small black beads. I pulled on my black leather boots and topped it off with my almost full-length black wool swing coat. This was Cassie's funeral and I wanted to look as nice as I possibly could.

I made the ten-minute drive to the funeral home, noticing the light snow that had accumulated on the ground. It was a beautiful afternoon, but I felt afraid and alone. As I drove, I asked God to give me the courage to do this. I prayed that this wasn't just my mind thinking that this was a good idea, but that this truly was an event of God's planning.

When I pulled into the parking lot of the funeral home, the number of cars that were there startled me. I knew there must be a couple hundred people inside. I was rapidly losing my courage. I began to doubt that there really would be a seat for me in that crowd.

As I walked to the entrance of the funeral home, I looked down at my all-black attire and became angry with myself for wearing such a ridiculous outfit. Everything about this was wrong, and I wanted to run the other way. I looked through the glass door inside and as I had feared, there was a large crowd of people milling about.

Just then someone opened the door. Standing there was a young man in an expensive-looking brown suit. His eyes were filled with kindness. He smiled at me and said, "Can I help you?"

I looked down at his nametag and to my surprise, I saw that the nametag read "Duane." I explained that I had talked with him just a few minutes earlier and gave him my name. He led me to the other room where there was already quite a crowd of mourners seated before an empty coffin. Duane took me to a long table in the back of the room where several ladies were seated writing the names of loved ones on gold colored Christmas ornaments.

An older woman gently asked, "What name would you like on your ornament?"

"Cassie," I said furtively, afraid someone might know that I was the reason Cassie was dead.

"Just Cassie, no last name?" the lady asked sympathetically.

"Just Cassie," this time the words came more confidently.

She wrote Cassie's name with a black marker on the gold surface. It was exciting to see someone write my daughter's name.

Duane led me back to the lobby where a huge Christmas tree stood already covered with hundreds of golden ornaments. He asked me where I would like the bulb hung. He never asked me any other questions. He somehow sensed my discomfort and didn't leave my side. When I asked him to place the bulb in a bare spot that was quite a stretch, he didn't complain.

He led me back to the room where the service was about to begin and found a seat for me near the front, next to an elderly couple. Then he disappeared.

I noticed a woman whose young son had been tragically and mysteriously killed the preceding winter. He was missing for quite a few days and all of us at the Christian TV station where I worked had been praying he'd be found alive. Sadly, after a few weeks his frozen little body had been found in a pond near his home. My heart ached for his mom.

Then I focused on the elderly couple next to me. They shared that they had lost quite a few friends of late and felt they needed to commemorate their lives. The gray-haired woman asked me if I had lost someone close to me.

"I lost a baby many years ago, and I have had a difficult time getting over it," I explained.

She nodded sympathetically and said she knew of someone else who had miscarried a baby and experienced a lot of grief. I felt compelled to tell her the truth about my abortion. I wanted to confess my sin, but thankfully the service started and I turned and gave my attention to the minister who was speaking.

The two ministers officiating related a few poignant stories and quoted several verses of Scripture. The first Scripture reading was from **Isaiah 40:1-5: "Comfort, comfort my people, says your God. Speak tenderly to Jerusalem, and proclaim to her that her hard service has been completed, that her sin has been paid for, that she has received from the Lord's hand double for all her sins." (Isaiah 40:1, 2 NIV)**

Looking at the words printed on the program seemed so odd. God had spoken these same words to me several times. In those moments when I was swallowed up in my grief, unable to forgive myself, He would remind me that the penalty of my sin had already been paid.

I had not paid it by my unrelenting self-abasement, but rather Jesus Christ had paid it with His shed blood on the Cross at Calvary. Not only had my sin been paid for, but God's Word assured me that His promise of restoration (**Step 2**) encompassed receiving twice what the enemy had stolen.

A lighting of a candle followed each Scripture. Since it was near Christmas, the succeeding Scriptures talked about Jesus coming to earth to save his children. The service was brief, and I can't remember feeling any deep emotion. Surprisingly, I did not shed a tear, although in my obedience to attend, I found a sense of release.

When the ceremony concluded, the elderly lady next to me asked compassionately, "Did it help?"

As I stood up to leave, I looked down at her and smiled. With genuine sincerity I said, "Yes." I wrapped the heavy black coat around me and as the other mourners were gathering for cookies and punch I headed for the front door.

There he was again, the compassionate funeral director. Duane was standing guard at the door just as he had been when I'd come in. Our eyes met and as they did, his eyes asked me the same question the elderly woman had asked me just moments before, "Did it help?"

The peaceful countenance that had replaced the apprehension I'd entered with was all the answer he needed. I gave the young man a smile of gratitude, and quietly whispered, "Thank you, Duane."

On the back of the program it said that ornaments could be picked up during the holiday season. I waited until New Year's Eve to pick up my precious ornament. I felt that Cassie's bulb should hang on the tree with all the other golden bulbs for as long as possible.

I returned for the ornament and left my car running since it was a cold day. The brisk air felt invigorating as I walked outside of the funeral home, clutching the ornament in my gloved hand. For the first time, someone had given me something that belonged to my daughter. This was Cassie's bulb. Cassie had actually lived for a short time on this earth. Now she was waiting for me in Heaven.

I cradled the bulb as a mother would cradle her infant. Finally I set the bulb down on the passenger seat next to me as though it were a fragile person with whom I'd been reunited. For the next few weeks I drove around with the ornament at my side.

CHAPTER EIGHT

TELLING MOM

"Confess your sins to each other...that you may be healed."
James 5:16 NIV

When you're little and you fall down and skin your knee, you run to your mama crying, wanting her comfort. She holds you and puts a bandage on your wound, whether you need it or not, then she assures you that you're loved.

I desperately wanted to tell my mom about my abortion, but I was too ashamed. It was a lot more than a cut on the knee, and because of her pro-life conviction, I thought there wouldn't be any words of love or comfort. One particular incident occurred when I was a young woman that convinced me that Mom might be unable to forgive me.

At the time, my mother was an avid volunteer for our local crisis pregnancy center manning the pro-life hotline that was forwarded to our home. One day when I was barely twenty I overheard her gently remark to someone on the phone, "You don't want to kill your baby, do you?"

Mom's subjective viewpoint really angered me. According to my pre-salvation philosophy, it wasn't a baby; it was only a glob of tissue. By overhearing her conversation, I surmised that the hotline was just a setup to get people to call to make a choice against abortion.

I am very ashamed to share this, but once I sabotaged one of the calls. I told a young woman struggling with a crisis pregnancy that she did have a choice. I didn't tell Mom about the call, because I was afraid of her reaction, but I did feel very self-righteous about my worldly advice.

I don't know if my mom's strong stand against abortion fueled my desire to join pro-choice. After all, I spent most of my troubled youth consumed with anger and rebellion. Simply because my mom said, "Abortion is wrong," might have been enough incentive for me to say that it was right.

Besides, what right did she have to tell people to keep their babies? All together, Mom had seven babies and one miscarriage. I was the eldest girl and five of my siblings were younger than me. By the time I was six-years-old, it was one of my duties to stand on a kitchen chair and wash dishes. When I wasn't much older I learned to cook dinner for eight. I resented that my childhood was swallowed up in caring for the needs of the other children, when I was still only a child myself.

Every time Mom had a baby, I took it as a personal affront. For me a baby meant more diapers and dishes to wash. It was also one more financial drain for an already impoverished family and one more thing for my parents to fight about.

Tidings of a new baby in Mom's womb brought tears to my eyes. They were not tears of joy, however, but rather tears of betrayal. *"How could she make my life more difficult than it already was?"* I thought.

This may sound very selfish, but children are selfish. I desperately wanted attention, and unfortunately as I grew I found attention through rebellion. My abortion was the ultimate rebellion, but it would have to remain hidden.

My secret held me in bondage so that I could not reach out for the forgiveness I needed. The very act of being secretive was retaining the shame of sin within my spirit and emotions. I knew this truth intellectually, yet I needed help in order to have the courage to tell Mom.

My help came in the form of another "mom" I happened to see while attending a county fair. I stopped at a gospel-singing tent and ended up sitting next to an elderly woman, who is a well-known author in our community. She knew I was also a writer, and that I had authored a biographical book about sexual abuse. Simply making conversation, she asked if I was working on another book.

"Yes, I am," I replied truthfully, dreading the next question that I was sure would follow.

"What's it about?" she asked without hesitation.

Oh, no. I was trapped, there appeared to be no way out. "It's about abortion," I said timidly, while praying that something would distract her.

"Is it your own story?" she continued matter-of-factly. Her tone suggested that she was not about to throw stones at me if I answered, "Yes."

"I had an abortion fourteen years ago. Unable to reconcile the guilt of my sin, I was driven to the Cross in need of a Savior," I replied truthfully.

She nodded her silver head knowingly. "My daughter had an abortion," she revealed. I heard pain in that woman's voice, pain for her daughter, and for the grandbaby that she never held in her arms.

I marveled at this Christian woman's compassion for her daughter. Was it possible that my mom would react the same way if she knew the truth? I had always believed that if my mom found out about the abortion, she would either be bitterly disappointed, or unable to forgive me. I was to discover her reaction sooner than I expected. The Bible gives us another prescription to produce healing after we have repented of our sin. **"...Confess your sins to each other and pray for each other so that you may be healed..." (James 5:16 NIV)**

I called my sister in Phoenix, who is often my confidant, and disclosed my plan to her. She tried to gently dissuade me from exposing the abortion to mom. Although, I usually listened to her advice, my mind was made up. **Step 7** of the healing process came in being willing to be honest. I had not only sinned against God and my baby, but I had sinned against my mother, as well.

Mom would be coming to Ohio for a visit in a few weeks. I started praying that God would prepare her heart for what she was about to learn. I was in the process of writing a book about abortion that would potentially touch thousands. How could I possibly keep it a secret any longer? I didn't want to hurt my mother, but I had to be honest if I was going to help others wounded by abortion.

The weekend of her visit arrived. I had prayed and asked several close friends to intercede that I would know God's exact moment to tell her.

On Saturday afternoon my mom and stepfather were coming for lunch. Before they arrived I paced and fretted and rehearsed what I would say. I wasn't sure if I should speak with Mom, if my stepdad was present? I was concerned that it would make the situation even more uncomfortable than I feared it would be.

In need of spiritual support, I called the local prayerline, and the precious volunteer prayed with me. She encouraged me to commit the situation to God, and to trust that He would show me exactly what to do.

I could barely eat any lunch. It was even more difficult to concentrate on our catching-up with family conversation. I was relieved when my stepfather retired into the living room to watch the football game.

Unexpectedly Mom said, "I need to go to the funeral home. A classmate of mine died, and I'm planning on meeting several other classmates there."

I silently thought, *"Oh, no, not now, Mom. I have to tell you something."* Then I had another thought: *"Maybe this was God's way of showing me that I really didn't need to tell her after all."*

Our lunch was the only time I would see her alone. Surely, I couldn't tell her at our family get-together that evening. Since they were returning to their home in Philadelphia in the morning, I reasoned that I must have originally missed God's voice.

Just then, my stepfather said, "Glenna, why don't you take Christina with you to the funeral home?"

My stepfather was trying to be polite and give us a little time together so that we could visit. Somehow, I think he sensed that I needed to talk with her alone.

The next thing I knew I was in the car with Mom fastening my seatbelt. I glanced down at my attire and realized that I had changed into the same black outfit that I had worn to Cassie's memorial service.

Mom pulled out of my driveway, and you guessed it, she headed toward Chiles and Sons-Laman Funeral Home, Shawnee Chapel. There are over a dozen funeral homes in our town, and I couldn't believe that we were driving to the one where I had ceremonially buried my daughter less than a month before.

As Mom drove, she chattered about her classmate, Dorothy, who had died. She was grateful that she would have an opportunity to pay her last respects. Mom was also excited to see her other classmates who were planning to meet her at the funeral home.

I felt sick to my stomach and my heart seemed to have somehow lodged in my throat. I could barely breathe. This was no time to tell her about Cassie.

En route to our destination, I sat silently in the car and prayed. When we reached the funeral home, I looked for my efficient funeral director, Duane Hinkle, but he was nowhere in sight.

Mom introduced me to some of her classmates and then we walked up and looked at Dorothy. My mother looked like a sad little girl as she stared at her friend lying in the casket. Before she could get too caught up in the sadness of the moment, her face lit up as she saw Dorothy's son, Randy.

Randy Williams or "Mort" as we had called him when we were young, was now a middle-aged man who was a funeral director himself. Dorothy had not only been Mom's classmate, but at one point they had been our neighbors. Her boys had also been my friends growing up. Randy always said he wanted to be a mortician, so that's how he ended up with the nickname, Mort. Now, he worked at Chiles and Sons Laman. That afternoon, he was polite and attentive, but I could see he was experiencing grief. We ran out of small talk quickly and Mom walked away and left me alone with Randy.

I told him that I was at the memorial service the preceding month and what a blessing it had been to me. Fortunately, Randy was either too immersed in his own grief or too professional to ask why I had attended the service. Despite our polite conversation, all I could think about was telling Mom.

Some of Mom's classmates decided to go for coffee. They invited both of us along. Our time together was drawing to a close and there we sat, drinking coffee and "oohing and aahing" over pictures of other people's grandchildren. There was never going to be a picture of my Cassie, which seemed to make the message I needed to tell Mom more urgent.

Finally, we were back in Mom's car driving in the direction of my home. Just a few more minutes and the door of opportunity would be closed. As she drove, I tried to tell Mom that I had a problem. The eternal optimist that she is, my mother brushed my concern aside and told me I didn't have a problem, that I was wonderful just the way I was.

We were within blocks of my house and I was frantic. I must have almost screamed, "Mom, I have to tell you something."

This jarred Mom out of her rose-tinted reality. She pulled the car over to the side of the road, screeching the tires as she applied the brakes a little too abruptly. She turned and looked at me, obviously confused.

"I've done something terrible, and I'm so sorry," I began. "But I have to tell you, because God wants me to help other people by writing a book. I can't keep it a secret any longer."

I saw her concerned eyes search my face for answers.

With tears streaming down my face, I said, "I had an abortion almost fifteen years ago."

Calmly, she replied matter-of-factly, "Don't you think I know that? You're my daughter."

"How could she know? How long had she known," I wondered.

I told her that I had no idea that she already knew. I explained about the depressions and not being able to get better and wanting to spare others from this terrible sin.

I further explained that I didn't think I could ever tell her because of her involvement in the pro-life movement. I said, "I know how much you hate abortion. I thought you'd hate me, too."

Without hesitating, she asked if I knew why she had spent so much time and energy working for the pro-life movement? I had always assumed it was because she hated abortion.

She looked at me very intently and said, "I know what it feels like to have to deal with a crisis pregnancy. If there's anything I can do to help you with your book, let me know. I would even be glad to write a chapter and explain why I worked for pro-life."

I always thought that Mom should write a book, so I decided to take her up on the offer.

CHAPTER NINE

MOM'S STORY
By Glenna Sprang

Today I'm blessed with a loving family, beautiful home, health and time to pursue my many interests. However, my life was difficult, raising five children in the 1950s and '60s. I suffered emotional, physical and economic traumas.

At times I lived with violence, neglect, abuse and poverty. When my children were young, I spent six weeks in a mental institution. After my divorce, I had to work three jobs to support my family.

Looking back on those turbulent years, I realize that although I lived with a man, cared for his children and created a home with him, emotionally there were very few times there was actually a "marriage." It was just the image of a good marriage. There was seldom a nurturing private life to support the public persona of the "happy couple."

When my fifth child was approximately two years old, I learned I was pregnant for the sixth time. Pregnancy is not the most comfortable condition in the world: morning sickness, fatigue, changes in your body, gaining weight, and then the trauma of giving birth, and pain that can last for days afterward.

Who would choose any of this except for love? Women say they forget the complications of pregnancy and the pain of childbirth, but I'm not sure that is true. We don't forget it, we are just willing to endure it, because we love our children and no pain is too much in light of that love.

I was never totally unhappy about being pregnant, because I was aware that God has a purpose for each life. However, it did overwhelm me, since I was in a situation where I doubted that I could properly care for the child.

I needed a good home and the means to help a child achieve his or her potential. I wanted to have the emotional, financial and physical resources to provide for a baby, and this was not always the case. In addition, I was always apprehensive about the actual pregnancy and delivery.

During my sixth pregnancy, I was feeling well. Then suddenly, at two and a half months, I had a miscarriage with complications, and I even lost the lining of my uterus. Although I was sad and weakened, there was a part of me that was grateful for not having to deal with the remaining seven months of the pregnancy, the painful delivery, and the responsibility of a new life.

As I experienced this partial sense of relief, I was not at all prepared for the total grief that would engulf me at the loss of this life. The grief weighed me down.

The physical implications of this miscarriage required that I be hospitalized. Later, my condition became so serious that I was hospitalized again, this time for corrective surgery. Although, I recovered and resumed my daily routine, my depression made life a colorless exercise. I was only able to pull myself out of this state when I was reminded that I had five healthy children who needed me.

It was at this time, I began to have such great compassion and sympathy for women who had aborted a child. I had a miscarriage and was dealing with such emptiness, that I couldn't imagine the kind of grief they were experiencing.

I often think of the child I miscarried forty years ago. In my mind, he was a blue-eyed blond boy, and I named him Tommy. I realized some years after the miscarriage that I would not have been able to properly care for him and for the two other children who were born to me later in life.

It has been said that a woman is asked to make a decision about carrying a child when she is not even in a state of mind to make a proper decision about what car to buy. The first three months of pregnancy are the most emotional and can attack the stability of the most well-adjusted woman. Unfortunately, women are pressured and put in the position of having to make decisions about a pregnancy in this state.

In some circumstances, an unwanted pregnancy can appear to put the well-being of present children in jeopardy. Many women are already working full-time to maintain a home, and do not have the ability to carry another child. In other instances, a woman fears rejection by her family, or sees plans for her education or career threatened.

It became important for me to help women dealing with this crisis in their lives, not just with words, but also with concrete support. Heartbeat, the local pro-life group where I volunteered, was typical of many organizations, private and church affiliated, which offer that support. There are non-violent, non-discriminatory groups whose sole purpose is to assist women and their children, born and unborn, regardless of age, race, or creed, in a practical, confidential manner. Our group would provide medical care, housing, clothes, emotional and material assistance.

Many times, it is in the best interest of the unborn child to allow that baby to be adopted, but this is a difficult decision to make. Even, if it is the most loving and unselfish course, it is extremely heartrending and sacrificial. How can women in a crisis pregnancy make decisions that are in everyone's best interest, if they do not have the support at the time they need it most?

Like most crisis pregnancy centers, Heartbeat did not stand in judgment of women who have had abortions. If we truly want to help someone, we cannot judge them, rather we must be there when and where they need us. Numerous crisis pregnancy centers nationwide, even have specific ministries for post-abortive women.

It has been many years since I actively worked for Heartbeat, but my compassion for pregnant women and those who have had abortions has only deepened. If you meet me today, you will see a woman who is in very comfortable circumstances, enjoys fashion, appears to be in glowing health, and only if you look very deeply into my eyes would you find any trace of the wounds of the past.

Gratitude is with me every moment. Gratitude to God, and to relatives and friends who helped me keep my family together. Special gratitude to my children, who are living their lives with love and courage, and have more than forgiven me for any hurts they suffered because of the choices I made. I can say with conviction that **Isaiah 41:10** is the truth: **"Fear thou not: for I am**

with thee: be not dismayed; for I am thy God: I will strengthen thee; yea, I will help thee." **(KJV)**

If you have had an abortion, don't allow this to become a destructive force in your life. Forgive yourself. You cannot change what is past, so you must accept it and go on with living and loving.

God does not want us weighted down with guilt, nor does He want us to use our energy punishing ourselves. Every minute we spend in shame and guilt, we've lost. Life is made up of these minutes, and we need to spend our time in loving, joyful, productive endeavors, honoring the God who loves us so much He sent His only Son.

If you are pregnant, and in difficult circumstances, please seek help. Call a church, a support group, or look in the Yellow Pages of the phone book for a crisis pregnancy center. Remember, the life you are carrying is not a "mistake," but a living, loving child. Don't assume you know how your family or the child's father will react. Whatever your circumstances may be, don't give up hope - hope for yourself, hope for your future, and hope for any children you may have.

No one can "fix" your life. Only you are responsible for the choices you make, but there are many people willing to help you. It will not be easy, and it will take courage. You have everything within you to lead a productive, happy life and see that your child lives to learn that "heaven and earth are full of His glory."

You will find beauty, if you look. Nothing is more beautiful than to look into a child's eyes.

CHAPTER 10

A SYNOPSIS OF THE STEPS

- **Step 1**: The Need for a Personal Relationship with Christ
- **Step 2**: The Promise of Restoration
- **Step 3**: Believing that Jesus looks after our little ones
- **Step 4**: Granting yourself permission to grieve
- **Step 5**: Forgive others/ Forgive yourself
- **Step 6**: Ceremony for Closure
- **Step 7**: Confessing to Others
- **Step 8**: Realized Restoration

Until the Spirit of the Lord reveals the horror of the sin of abortion, and sends His conviction into the hearts of men, little will change. **Romans 2:4 NIV** says, **"Or do you show contempt for the riches of his kindness, tolerance and patience, not realizing that God's kindness leads you towards repentance?"** The second half of the Scripture in the **KJV** reads, **"...not knowing that the goodness of God leadeth thee to repentance?"**

It is not condemnation, but conviction often brought about by God's goodness, that brings sinners to repentance. Since we see God through the actions of others, it is important that the Church react as Christ would towards those contemplating abortion, and those who have already committed this sin. One of the Church's greatest challenges is to extend grace to those in the Body of Christ suffering from the long-term effects of abortion.

Years ago, God ministered this grace to me on the twelfth anniversary of my abortion in December 1995. He gave me a promise through His Word that He was going to heal me of my emotional pain from the thirtieth chapter of Jeremiah. **"For thus saith the Lord, Thy bruise is incurable, and the wound is grievous."** (Jeremiah 30:12 KJV)

God witnessed the terrible pain that abortion had brought into my life. He saw that without His divine intervention, my situation

91

was hopeless. The incurable wound or pain of abortion comes from realizing the heinous crime that you have committed by taking the life of your own child.

"There is none to plead thy cause, that thou mayest be bound up: thou hast no healing medicines." (Jeremiah 30:13 KJV)

There is no person or drug upon this earth that can fix the heartbreak abortion brings. **"All thy lovers have forgotten thee; they seek thee not; for I have wounded thee with the wound of an enemy, with the chastisement of a cruel one, for the multitude of thine iniquity; because thy sins were increased."** (Jeremiah 30:14 KJV) In the New International version this same verse reads: **"I have struck you as an enemy would and punished you as would the cruel, because your guilt is so great and your sins so many."** God let me know that although my sin had been pleasurable for a season it eventually brought death into my life as the **"wages of sin is death...."** (Romans 6:23 KJV)

Jeremiah 30:15 NIV continues, **"Why do you cry out over your wound, your pain that has no cure? Because of your great guilt and many sins I have done these things to you."**

My abortion brought the literal death of an innocent human being. It also created a kind of death in my soul that only those who have committed this sin can probably understand. God admits that He allowed me to be wounded as a **chastisement,** from the Hebrew *muwcar* (1) meaning reproof, warning, correction or rebuke, so that I could be brought to repentance.

"But all who devour you will be devoured; all your enemies will go into exile. Those who plunder you will be plundered; all who make spoil of you I will despoil." (Jeremiah 30:16 NIV)

Despite Israel's great guilt, God later promises in this same verse, that He will take care of her enemies. He promises this, also, to those of us who has fallen into the sin of abortion. This passage closes with another promise, one of God's restoration. **"But I will restore you to health and heal your wounds, because you are called an outcast, Zion for whom no one cares."** (Jeremiah 30:17 NIV)

In Chapter 3, **The Promise of Restoration** is listed as **Step 2** of the healing process, because of its spiritual importance. In order for God to have the ability to restore in our lives, all eight steps of the healing process need to occur. **Step 1) The Need for Personal Relationship with Christ** must take place before any of the other steps can be fully accomplished, because apart from Him there is only limited healing available. (Step 1 is prayerfully outlined in the last chapter.)

Restoration is often a twofold promise combining both **Step 2) The Promise of Restoration and Step 8) Restoration Realized.** (Step 8 is fully defined in Chapter 12.) For an example, let's refer back to "Katie," my ministerial co-worker. Katie disclosed to her fellow ministry workers that she had an abortion, which left her with emotional scars that needed God's healing. What Katie didn't reveal was that her physical health was also affected by the abortion.

Later, when we were alone, she told me about the fear that kept her from getting adequate medical treatment following the procedure. Poor Katie was only seventeen when she terminated her unwanted pregnancy. She was terrified that the horrible secret of her abortion would somehow be disclosed if she sought follow-up treatment.

Most of us were like Katie. We were too ashamed to go for help. One of the most dramatic examples of this occurred decades ago. It is the infamous case of Jane Doe, who made national news when she bled to death in a hotel room after a botched abortion. This unidentified young woman died after aborting a child and receiving no follow-up care.(2)

Katie's medical consequences were not as life threatening. Following her abortion, her need for forgiveness led her back to Christ. She eventually married and had several beautiful children. She feels these children were truly a blessing from God that expressed His restorative ability and forgiving grace. Unfortunately, Katie also had to undergo a hysterectomy in her late twenties.

Like Katie, statistics report that 200,000 women annually experience physical complications following an abortion.(3) They can also be dishonest with their doctors about their medical history, because of their shame. Therefore, we cannot precisely track the number of women whose lives have been altered by inadequate medical care.

One survey conducted by the "AIS Project" reports that long-term physical complications of abortion include: 1) infertility by 8 percent or 89 of 1,145 women, 2) hemorrhage by 9 percent of the women, and 3) over 70 percent of the women surveyed were affected by emotional problems including guilt, depression, and remorse.(4) In a study conducted in Sweden, approximately 60 percent of women questioned, claimed that they experienced emotional distress following their abortion. The emotional distress was classified as severe in 30 percent of those surveyed.(5)

The widely acclaimed _Archives of General Psychiatry_ reports that a large number of women are plagued with a condition known as Post Traumatic Stress Disorder following an abortion. Specific symptoms of PTSD revealed through the research include; insomnia, general numbing, and nightmares or flashbacks.(6) A Finnish study conducted to track the suicide rate of women after pregnancy also revealed a frightening statistic. "The suicide rate after an abortion was three times the general suicide rate and six times that associated with birth."(7)

I personally experienced some of the above symptoms including suicidal tendencies. Later, I recognized that many of my emotional problems stemmed from an inability to accept God's forgiveness. How could I call on God when I had done such a terrible thing? And yet, as I wrote in an earlier chapter, when I cried out to Him, He would reassure me that He had not only forgiven my sin, but that it was forgotten."**And their sins and iniquities will I remember no more.**" (Hebrews 10:17 KJV)

True repentance involves not only being sorry for the sin you have committed, but earnestly hating the sin itself, and seeing how truly vile and unholy it is before God.

According to the "AIS Project" survey, 76 percent of the women polled said they would not have an abortion if given the chance to undo their mistake.(8) It is important to note, however, that because of the nature of abortion, statistics can be very one-sided.

Therefore, for the purpose of journalistic accuracy, we also refer back to the _Archives of General Psychiatry_ representing, what could possibly be a more general population survey. In this study, 31 percent of the participants acknowledged that they were either not sure, or definitely certain that they would not have an abortion again.(9)

Regardless of which statistic is accurate, it is apparent that many post-abortive men and women regret their decision. This hurting population often chooses substance abuse to numb their emotional pain. Dr. David Reardon documented this fact in 2000 in the <u>American Journal of Drug and Alcohol Abuse</u>. This report portrays an alarming five to one ratio of substance abuse in women who are post-abortive, as compared to women who carried their pregnancy to term.(10)

Unfortunately, it is humanly impossible to undo an abortion. However, it is possible to repent and have Christ's blood pay the full penalty for whatever sin we commit.

Since we are a triune being: spirit, soul, and body, true repentance must occur in all three areas. The soul of man consists of the intellect, the will, and the emotions. Genuine repentance begins in the intellect. We feel sorrow and contrition resulting in a "change of mind" about our action. The "change of mind" transmits to the area of the will, which causes an actual change of heart, ultimately resulting in repentance within our emotions.

We need to avoid the danger of getting stuck in the third stage of repentance. Our emotions can become consumed by the horror of our action, once we come to know Christ and realize the deception of the enemy.

"Godly sorrow brings repentance that leads to salvation and leaves no regret, but worldly sorrow brings death. See what this godly sorrow has produced in you: what earnestness, what longing, what concern, what readiness to see justice done." (II Cor. 7:10 & 11 NIV)

Repentance is a gift from God that allows our hardened conscience to become open to His voice and the need for His forgiveness and salvation. I spent years consumed by an emotional grief that was not Godly sorrow, but rather the sorrow of the world, which leads to death.

I accepted the lie that my baby was dead, when in reality we learned in **Step 3** (Chapter 4) **Our Babies are Alive and Living with Jesus in Heaven.** Not only are they alive, but also God can show us the name and sex of our child through prayer.

Step 4 (Chapter 5) **Granting Yourself Permission to Grieve** must not be confused with wallowing in guilt, because as Christians we do not grieve like the world.

"Brothers, we do not want you to be ignorant about those who fall asleep, or to grieve like the rest of men who have no hope. We believe that Jesus died and rose again and so we believe that God will bring with Jesus those who have fallen asleep in him." (I Thessalonians 4:13 & 14 NIV)

For some involved in the sin of abortion it is necessary to pray that the gift of repentance will come. The enemy can cause us to justify and rationalize our involvement, or to convince us that there truly was no other way out. Abortion is never justified and never an acceptable way to deal with a crisis pregnancy, but it is forgivable.

Once I realized that God required that I **Forgive Others Step 5** (Chapter 6) in order to receive His forgiveness, it became necessary to make a disciplined decision to forgive myself. God wants you to give yourself the gift of forgiveness, also.

God is not only the God of forgiveness, but He is the God of the second chance, and the third, fourth, or however many chances we need. Sometimes, when people's hearts have become hardened they undergo several abortions. This might be especially true for the sin of abortion, since guilt often does not come immediately. For many men and women involved in this sin, it surfaces years later when they have children of their own, desire to start a family, or find themselves in changed circumstances spiritually, financially, or even emotionally. When these individuals accept Christ, they look at the magnitude of their sin. They think that there is hope for someone else to have complete forgiveness, but not for them.

According to data gathered by the Centers for Disease Control and Prevention, 54 percent of women who obtained an abortion did so for the first time. About 26 percent had one previous abortion, around 18 percent had at least two previous abortions, and 2 percent were unknown.(11)

Remember **Hosea 4:2** says, **"bloodshed follows bloodshed."** In verse six of this Scripture, Hosea explains why: **"My people are destroyed from lack of knowledge."** (**Hosea 4:6 NIV**)

Abortion is no different than any other sin. Until God reveals and convicts that abortion is the murder of an innocent, often this sin will be repeated. Women who have had multiple abortions must accept forgiveness by faith in Christ's blood, like anyone else guilty of any repetitive sin.

For those of you who have had an abortion or multiple abortions **Step 6** includes a **Ceremony for Closure** of your grieving. Your babies are real people safe in the Father's loving arms. No matter how many babies you have aborted, you have God's permission to grieve this loss.

Not only does God give you permission to grieve, but you must go through grief's various stages according to Step 4, in order to become healed. God's healing grace will lead you through this time, if you ask for His help. Our Heavenly Father sent His son Jesus Christ to **"...comfort all who mourn, and provide for those who grieve in Zion,** (the church) **to bestow on them a crown of beauty instead of ashes, the oil of joy instead of mourning, and a garment of praise instead of the spirit of despair."** (**Isaiah 61:2 & 3 NIV**)

Right now some of you might be angry that I am extending mercy to women like myself, who have taken the life of innocent children. I once talked to a friend who said, "I feel if someone takes someone else's life, then they should have to pay for that with their own life."

She was not referring to abortion, but rather to the crime of murder in general. This normally merciful lady knows I have struggled greatly in becoming the whole person God intends.

Before I knew what I was doing, I blurted out that I understood how she felt, but that I was also a murderer not deserving of life. I then shared with her that I had an abortion and that is why it had been so difficult for me to see myself as forgiven and accepted by Christ. She began to minister to me about the power of forgiveness available through Christ's blood.

The Church, as a whole, has not extended forgiveness to those guilty of the sin of abortion. As was mentioned earlier, Step 5 of the healing process comes through forgiving others so that we can be forgiven. Whether we have had an abortion or some other sin, as humans we all continually need Christ's forgiveness.

Step 7 of healing from abortion requires **Confessing to Others** in the body of Christ. Remember **James 5:16 NIV** says, **"Confess your sins to each other and pray for each other so that you may be healed"** — not so that you can be judged. Disclosing our sin to those who heap further condemnation on us can be devastating. Therefore, we must use great wisdom in choosing a confidant. Besides, a law of judgment is enacted over the lives of those who accuse others to the Father, instead of extending to them the mercy and forgiveness that Christ purchased for all of us at Calvary.

To illustrate this spiritual truth let's study **Matthew 18:22-35**. To condense this passage, we learn of two servants and a king. The first servant owes the king a debt that in today's terms would amount to millions of dollars. He begs the king for mercy, which the king shows by canceling the huge debt and letting him go. This is an example of the final step to our healing **Step 8) Realized Restoration**. (see last chapter)

The pardoned servant, however, went out to find one of his fellow servants who still owed him a debt of only a few dollars. Unlike the merciful king who pardoned him, he refuses to be patient and has the indebted servant thrown into prison. When the king heard of this unfair treatment, he was angry. Thus Scripture states that the pardoned servant forfeited his own restoration by judgment of another. **"Then the master called the servant in. 'You wicked servant,' he said, 'I canceled all the debt of yours because you begged me to. Shouldn't you have had mercy on your fellow servant just as I had on you?' In anger his master turned him over to the jailers to be tortured, until he should pay back all he owed. This is how my heavenly Father will**

treat each of you unless you forgive your brother from your heart." (Matthew 18:32-35 NIV)

As children of God, and brothers and sisters in the Lord, we need the forgiveness and understanding of others when we fall, whether through abortion or any other sin. I am reminded of a young female soldier from West Virginia, who fell into enemy hands during the War in Iraq in 2003. Fellow soldiers from several branches of the armed forces united in a successful attempt to free 19-year-old Jessica Lynch from an Iraqi hospital where she was being held prisoner. One of the soldiers remarked that "we don't leave a fallen comrade behind."

At the time, I thought how appropriate this soldier's statement was in spiritual terms. Although Lynch has reported that the Iraqis offered no resistance, still our U.S. military men risked their lives for the freedom of a seemingly unimportant comrade. Are we willing to do the same, to see that the "least of these" is restored to Christ? After all, at the Last Judgment we will stand before our Heavenly King and He will say, **"I tell you the truth, whatever you did for one of the least of these brothers of mine, you did for me." (Matthew 25:40 NIV)**

CHAPTER 11

TELLING THE WORLD

Telling Mom about the abortion had turned out to be the right thing to do. Now, I needed the courage to tell the world.

The week of talk shows I helped to produce on the 25th anniversary of Roe vs. Wade prepared me to do exactly that. All the testimonies that week were from women who had either had an abortion, been encouraged to have an abortion, or had been prevented from having one.

One particular guest stands out in my mind. She had an abortion and began to hemorrhage, which later caused her to undergo a hysterectomy. Besides the physical aftermath, she also suffered terrible grief. God eventually gave her a vision of her child, and assured her of His forgiveness, just as He had done for me.

She had a zeal for telling anyone who would listen, how the trauma of abortion had affected her. After her segment was over, we sat on the couch of our interview set and wept together. Talking about the hurts of the past can sometimes make us revisit the pain momentarily. Perhaps that's why we frantically avoid confronting the past, fearing the pain. Yet, with each tear shed, each memory relived, and each secret disclosed appropriately, we are closer to total freedom in Christ.

This young woman was on a mission, and she didn't care how much it cost her emotionally. She worked for a crisis pregnancy center spending her days combating the "demon" of abortion.

I'm sure others thought I was simply being a comforting producer to an upset guest as I wrapped my arms around her. With tears streaming down her face, she said something like, "We have to tell people. We have to speak up. They need to know the truth about abortion."

She had just exposed her life to thousands of people. She didn't know that she had done it for me. She had taken my place on the interview set that day, because I was not ready. I was afraid of what people would think, and afraid of tapping into the grief that I still found unbearable.

She reminded me so much of Christ as He hung on the cross dying for my sin, taking the shame for me, not worrying about what others thought of Him. As I held her, I told her she had great courage. I now realize that it was more than courage. It was a kind of desperation God was using to expose the deception of Satan.

I did break down and tell her that I had also had an abortion and that was why I so admired her ability to tell her story. She looked at me with a kind of resignation I did not understand at the time. It was only later when the same zeal to expose the enemy consumed me that I understood. When you are vocal about having had an abortion you will meet many women who have also experienced the same trauma. They will tell you of their pain, and shame. Sometimes, they will tell you how God has healed them, but then they will add that they could never tell anyone else. They'll explain about the husband that doesn't know, the children that have never been told, or the parents who would disapprove.

Things will not change unless we speak up and let the world know how traumatic the consequences of abortion are. Nevertheless, I also nod empathetically now, when someone shares why they could never reveal their secret to others. It is a personal choice and one must be led by God's Spirit and His timing. In order to effect change, however, the combined voice of our outcry needs to be heard by the world. If that does not happen, there will be only isolated pleas for help. Change will not take place until the day when post-abortive women unite and say, "Enough is enough."

It was time to tell the world, I needed to begin with my sphere of associates. I decided to start by confessing to those with whom I worked closely in ministry. One day, following morning devotions, a group of about twelve of my ministerial co-workers gathered. I briefly shared my pain from the sin of abortion. Instantly, I sensed that these normally gregarious people were uncomfortable and at a loss for words.

I made my disclosure and asked for the prayers of others concerning what I felt called to do. I shared that I believed God wanted me to write a book and to begin speaking about the aftermath of my own abortion. There was a deafening silence in the room. No one said anything, I'm sure for fear of saying the wrong thing.

When I left the small meeting, a male staff person patted me on the shoulder, the way a ball player consoles his buddy when he has just fumbled an important play. That little gesture meant a lot to me. Later that day, a female co-worker hugged me in the hallway, which was somewhat out of character for her, but greatly appreciated.

The most interesting attempt to help me came in the form of a book, "*Post-Abortion Trauma*" by Jeanette Vought. (1) The book somehow found its way to the top of the papers on my cluttered desk that afternoon. I wish there would have been a note attached, or inscription saying "I'm praying for you." This anonymity caused my own sin consciousness to shame me into feeling that I was the leper that had been found out.

The incident demonstrated to me that for the post-abortive woman there is often little help available, even from those in ministry. At least employed as a producer and reporter for a Christian talk show, I received a pat, hug and a book to encourage me. I wondered what support other hurting women would find in their own spiritual circle. Despite this fact, God always sends us help in His way, when we ask. **"Call unto me, and I will answer thee, and show thee great and mighty things, which thou knowest not." (Jeremiah 33:3 KJV)**

While I was producing the Roe vs. Wade shows to minister and educate others, some of my own answers came. The research I did for the series led me to discover some interesting people whose lives had been touched by abortion, and who now work for pro-life. One such person was Sydna Massé, president of Ramah International, a post abortion ministry.

Sydna is also the author of the book, "Her Choice to Heal: Finding Spiritual and Emotional Peace After an Abortion." (2)

Sydna referred me to a ministry in Cincinnati, which has resources to aid in the healing of post-abortive women. Sydna also shared her personal experience from the pain of abortion with me. She too had a passion to tell others.

The ministry she referred me to is known as H.E.A.R.T., which stands for Helping and Educating in Abortion Related Trauma. Through a phone conversation, I met two precious women, Rose Diemler, founder of the post-abortion ministry, and Cinny Roy, the current director. Although Rose has never had an abortion, she has been greatly used of God to heal the wounds of others. She has conducted many post-abortion Bible studies that have helped women, men, and teens to find wholeness. Rose has authored a book to assist others to facilitate Bible studies for the post-abortive. (3)

Cinny Roy has experienced the heartbreak of abortion, and made the decision to speak publicly about the aftermath. Both of these women consented to share their stories for our Roe vs. Wade television series. When I met these two ladies, I felt like I had truly met sisters in Christ. Before we began the shows, I disclosed to them concerning my own abortion and my desire to touch others who were hurting. I shared that I had not yet publicly spoken of my abortion, but I was scheduled to speak at a church the following Sunday. Since it was Sanctity of Life Sunday, I felt it was God's plan that I tell my story to the congregation for the first time.

Rose and Cinny were so encouraging, and they assured me they would be praying for me. Cinny prepared me for a few things that I should expect. She said that some women might bolt from the sanctuary and not be able to listen because of the pain in their own past.

I heard this same scenario from Katie my ministerial associate whose initial disclosure about her abortion helped to fuel the vision for this book. She also discussed her phobia of attending church on Sanctity of Life Sunday. Katie said that her pain and shame would often drive her to the church bathroom, until the annual abortion sermon would come to a close.

Katie and I agreed that we would probably meet a lot of our fellow sufferers in the church bathroom during this special Sunday. I purposed in my heart to be especially sensitive to these women when I shared my story.

That Sunday, when I spoke about my abortion and its painful aftermath, a few women wept. A couple of people in the pews looked pretty horrified, which was difficult to not interpret as judgment. Most just appeared perplexed as though they had little understanding regarding abortion. These reactions only made me more intense, since my desire was to educate the church to assist women trapped in crisis pregnancy.

It was not a very encouraging evening. At home that night, confused as to whether I had made the right choice to disclose publicly, I called a friend who had been praying for the service. I told him that it was not a very receptive audience and I wondered if my message had been of any value.

He countered, "But did you get an Amen from heaven, Sister?" Instantly, I realized that it didn't matter how people responded. My obedience to the Lord was all that was important.

A short time later, I met a very well known woman through another phone conversation. She encouraged me to continue my path to disclose the deception about abortion.

Many Americans may be unfamiliar with the name Norma McCorvey, but they readily recognize "Jane Roe." Norma McCorvey was Jane Roe. Jane Roe was the defendant named in the infamous Supreme Court decision that legalized abortion in the U.S. on Jan. 22, 1973.

I use "was" Jane Roe because Norma McCorvey became a new creature in Christ in 1995. Victimized for years as a reluctant poster child for the pro-choice movement, Norma never even had an abortion. Her testimony of God's grace in changing her life is completely explained in her book, "Won by Love." (4)

There were several times when I felt I absolutely could not continue with the task of publicly disclosing my own pain of abortion. It was then, I would receive a brief note from Miss Norma. I saw God's divine providence in the few correspondences I received from her. Once, her assistant and friend, Connie Gonzales sent me the gift of "Won by Love" on a day when I needed God's encouragement the most.

Miss Norma, as she prefers to be called, was one of Satan's pawns in his great plan to destroy millions of babies through the sin of abortion. She also spent years working inside an abortion clinic seeing firsthand the horror of abortion on a day-to-day basis. Now, through her ministry, **Roe No More**, she travels the country telling others of Christ's love, which has dramatically changed her life.

Unfortunately, many hurting women and men are still becoming victims of abortion mills because they do not know Christ's love. In 1995, 19 percent of all U.S. pregnancies ended in abortion. The 1995 abortion statistic, which is the highest rate of abortion for any Western industrialized country, is alarming even to those who are proponents of the procedure.(5) More recent statistics also continue to be alarming regarding the use of abortion as a means of contraception. In 2003, the Ohio Right to Life Website indicated that 93% of abortions are performed as a means of birth control.

Most pro-choice advocates support making contraceptives affordable and available, and increasing sex education in the schools. Ms. McCorvey feels that God has a better remedy for this. She was once quoted as saying, "I'd like young women to understand that abortion is not the ultimate answer (to an unwanted pregnancy). The answer is in counseling and Christian fellowship."(6)

Norma McCorvey was not the last person who God would choose to lead me in my endeavor to reach those devastated by abortion. In April of 2001, I met another woman whose love portrayed a living example of Christ. Many would recognize Kathy Troccoli as a famous Christian recording artist, however, I will always remember her as a "Lady of Love."

It was my privilege to interview Ms. Troccoli when I served in ministry as a Christian television reporter. During those years, I was blessed to interview "celebrities" occasionally. I intentionally use quotation marks around the term "celebrity" as most of the precious people I met thought of themselves as servants, rather than stars. There are several who stand out in my mind even now. I will never forget the kindness of Larnelle Harris as he waited patiently in 95-degree heat while I searched for my missing cameraman in the vast crowd. Then there was Sandy Patti who touched my heart, because of her honesty about God's ability to keep us through our mistakes. Chonda Pierce and Liz Curtis Higgs made me laugh and cry all at the same time, while the purity exuded by Rebecca St. James gave me great hope.

There were others, who were special, too, but it was spending twenty minutes with Kathy Troccoli, that helped me find the courage to complete this book. Her recording of a "Baby's Prayer" and her work in the pro-life movement were the reason I interviewed her that spring evening. She told me insightfully, "Secrets make you sick." I've thought about that truth a great deal, while completing this book. Like so many post-abortive women, I have been fearful of exposing my past. I didn't want to shame my husband or son, or have people look at me differently. More important than how people view me though, is my desire to be used of God to help others heal and to spare the lives of the innocent.

This award winning Christian musician was so compassionate and non-judgmental, I assumed that she must be post-abortive, too. I was surprised when she answered that she was not. She felt called to reach those of us, who were broken and ashamed, and often without hope. She has spent a great deal of her time ministering to this hurting population. Through meeting her I realized that I, too, needed to spend time helping my wounded sisters and brothers.

When asked, what lasting impression she would like to leave when her time on this earth has past? Kathy Troccoli remarked that she would like to be remembered as a "Lady of Love," and that is how I will always think of her.

CHAPTER 12

ANOTHER CASSIE

In order to have compassion for the victims of abortion, we need to personalize this legal holocaust. Once we put a face on abortion, it becomes an entirely different matter. There are concerned legislators and dedicated pastors who have risked their reputations due to their strong stand for pro-life. It is time that those of us who have been victimized by this hideous legal method of destruction pray for the courage to unite our voices to spare the next generation. As post-abortive men and women, we know intimately the devastating details concerning abortion.

I hesitated to address this issue earlier, because I feared I would sound like a nagging malcontent who desires to blame my poor choice of abortion on others. I assure you, I take full accountability for my sin, but I will probably go to my grave wondering, "What if?"

What if a protester outside of the clinic on the day of my abortion would have lovingly said, "I want your baby. I'll help you get through this, then raise your child." Had I been offered a compassionate option to abortion, would that have swayed my decision to go through with the procedure? I'll never know.

Before I was vocal about the fact I had an abortion, Christians would come to me wanting praise because they had been arrested on an abortion protest line. I would usually just walk away saying nothing. How could I praise them for doing nothing, just as it seemed to me all those demonstrators had done the day I unknowingly murdered my daughter?

A decade ago, my Biblical belief that action must accompany faith was sorely tested. A young female acquaintance, who is HIV positive, had found out that she was pregnant. Definitely not planning this pregnancy, she panicked and contemplated abortion.

At the time, I was raising a teenager alone. My schedule was overcome with operating a thrift store ministry, completing a book about sexual abuse, and doing it all on a non-existent budget. I was also rapidly approaching my fortieth birthday.

In the past, I had mentally criticized others for not assisting women trapped by crisis pregnancy in a tangible way. I tried to rationalize that this was a sick baby and it would be too much responsibility for me at this stage of my life. I prayed that God would call upon someone else who would rise to the occasion. However, when I prayed I was burdened with the thought that if no one offered to help, the little one's life might be taken.

I also realized that I needed to live my faith. Therefore, I made a decision to offer to take the unborn infant. In God's Divine Providence, the very day of that decision, the mother resolved in her heart that abortion was not an option. No matter what, she would give birth and raise the child herself. I'm happy to say that today that precious child tests negative for the HIV virus, and the mother is still healthy, too.

A number of years ago, Pastor Marc Curry, past-president of the ministerial association in Lima, Ohio, gave me a prophetic "word" from the Lord. He said that God had spoken specifically that I was "to take care of the Lord's babies."

Pastor Curry was unaware that at the time, I was producing a video package about the significant increase of pregnant mothers addicted to drugs. In my hometown of Lima with a population of less than 50,000 residents, local neonatalogist Dr. Vincente Romero expressed concern in this feature over the fact that between ten and twenty percent of babies born in Allen county were born to mothers who were using drugs.(1)

He was desperate for people to learn about this frightening statistic, because he realized that at-risk expectant moms need education and support to birth healthy babies who would one day be productive adults. This interview only confirmed my belief that Satan tries diligently to kill a child from the moment of conception. If he can't get a woman to abort, he continues to try to destroy the child through drugs. Cocaine babies have a very real chance of having congenital brain, heart or kidney problems that severely alter their hopes for a productive life. (2)

Armed with knowledge about Satan's plan to destroy babies, it became somewhat easier to speak about abortion. Several months later, it was again Sanctity of Life Sunday and I was speaking in a church out of state. I shared about my abortion and following that meeting six people approached me and shared how they had each been involved in abortion. They had either had an abortion or taken someone they loved for the procedure. One woman had three abortions, and was still greatly in need of healing. I could see remorse and pain as they confessed their sin. I could also see the gratitude in their eyes knowing they were not alone.

When we sin unknowingly and later repent, God takes our sin and pain and turns it into something beautiful. This is the final step in receiving God's wholeness. **Step 8) Realized Restoration** is achieved when the promise of restoration that we have lived for, becomes reality in our lives.

We see an example of God's forgiveness and restoration in the life of King David. David committed adultery with Bathsheba, the wife of Uriah the Hittite. Bathsheba soon conceives David's child, and in order to cover up their sin, David has Bathsheba's husband killed in battle. Nathan the prophet reveals to David that because of his sins of adultery and murder, the Lord's judgment is about to come upon him.

"The Lord has taken away your sin. You are not going to die. But because by doing this you have made the enemies of the Lord show utter contempt, the son born to you will die."

After Nathan had gone home, the Lord struck the child that Uriah's wife had borne to David, and he became ill. David pleaded with God for the child. He fasted and went into his house and spent the nights lying on the ground. The elders of his house stood beside him to get him up from the ground, but he refused and he would not eat any food with them.

On the seventh day the child died." (II Samuel 12:13-18 NIV)

David's servants were afraid to tell him the child was dead, because of the way he had earnestly sought the Lord for the child's life. However, David realized the baby was dead, because of the way the servants were acting. When it was verified that his son had died, David did a very strange thing. **"Then David got up from the ground.** **After he had washed, put on lotions and changed his clothes, he went into the house of the Lord and worshipped. Then he went to his own house, and at his request they served him food and he ate."** (II Samuel 12:20 NIV) In light of the way David acted before the infant's death, this abnormal behavior really confused the servants. They thought that if his baby died, David's grief would overcome him. Through the Scriptures David offers an explanation of his behavior to those of his household: **"While the child was still alive, I fasted and wept. I thought, 'Who knows? The Lord may be gracious to me and let the child live.' But now that he is dead, why should I fast? Can I bring him back again? I will go to him, but he will not return to me? And David comforted his wife, and went to her, and lay with her. She gave birth to a son, and they named him Solomon."** (II Samuel 12:23 & 24 NIV)

Like David, I couldn't bring my Cassie back, but one day I will go to her. I did not birth a Solomon, a son of restoration: but my **Step 8) Realized Restoration** has come through birthing many spiritual children. I also asked God for the grace to accept that my daughter was gone and to use our story to touch others.

I never stop feeling a momentary twinge of recognition when I hear someone say the name "Cassie." It is as if all the Cassies on the earth belong to me. In April 1999, my heart broke for a family from Colorado who also lost their Cassie.

As the news feed of the tragic shootings at Columbine High School in Littleton, Colorado poured into the TV station, one student who was killed stood out because of her name. I watched with horror as a beautiful blue-eyed blonde named Cassie Bernall was listed among the victims.

As Cassie was studying Shakespeare in the school library, Dylan Klebold and Eric Harris conducted their bloody rampage leaving 13 dead. Nationwide, the media reported that one of the killers pointed a gun at Cassie and asked her if she believed in God. Cassie answered, "Yes," knowing it would probably cost her life. In that instant the young man fired and sent Cassie into eternity to be with her Savior.

Cassie Bernall paid the ultimate price for believing in Christ. Perhaps, the reason I identify with her most was that she had not always believed in Jesus as her Savior. Just a few years earlier she dabbled in witchcraft and was obsessed with suicide. Then she had a radical conversion and became a spokesperson for the God she once shunned.(3) Cassie was a teenager with dreams and goals, and with a family who loved her. Her family is left behind and I suspect that even years later, they are still trying to make sense out of what seems like a senseless tragedy.

As the entire nation mourned for the Columbine students, my thoughts centered on a Cassie whom I had never met. I thought how proud her parents must be, and yet, how their pride in their daughter's courageous conviction could not possibly numb the horror of the grief of the tragic loss of her life.

It became obvious, too, that children are truly just on loan to us from our heavenly Father. We never know when we will have to relinquish them back into His hands.

Sin destroyed the life of Cassie Bernall. It was not her sin, rather it was the sin of two troubled teenagers who turned themselves over to the enemy to be used as instruments of destruction. **"For we wrestle not against flesh and blood, but against principalities, against powers, against the rulers of the darkness of this world, against spiritual wickedness in high places. Wherefore take unto you the whole armour of God, that ye may be able to withstand in the evil day, and having done all, to stand." (Ephesians 6:12 KJV)**

At the time of the Columbine shootings some pro-life advocates linked abortion to the fact that the school shootings had occurred. How could legalized abortion be responsible for the bloody rampage committed by two troubled teens? Quite simply, our country's stance on abortion causes our young people to see how expendable human life has become to us as a nation.

According to a statement issued by Cassie's parents at her funeral, Cassie made her decision to stand despite the consequence. "Her life was rightly centered around our Lord Jesus. It was for her strong faith in God and His promise of eternal life that she made her stand," said the Bernalls.(4)

Cassie Bernall is a modern day martyr for the Christian faith. I would like to believe that my daughter would have been courageous like her. She was a martyr, too, only my Cassie was killed simply for being conceived. The 2003 Right to Life web site states that currently approximately 1,300,000 babies are aborted each year. This figure translates to 3,300 abortions being performed each day in U.S. abortion clinics. Yet, we are not fighting people or politics. We are actually fighting the spirit of murder, which Satan has assigned to destroy our children.

The greatest weapon the enemy has used against me personally is sin-consciousness. Making me so conscious of my sin and the subsequent grief that he tried to block my faith for tomorrow. He wants to hold you in that bondage, too, but remember in **II Samuel 12:23** David said, **"I will go to him, but he will not return to me,"** referring to the son he lost.

In a natural sense we will not see our aborted babies on this earth. We will have to be like Cassie Bernall's parents and all the millions of others who have buried children in the Lord, and wait for a joyous reunion in heaven.

Somewhere in Colorado, there is a gravestone that belongs to Cassie Bernall. No, Cassie isn't there, she's with the Jesus that she was willing to die for. However, her family and friends can go there and remember this precious girl by taking her flowers or a special memento.

In July of 2001, I was blessed to find that a resting place for my Cassie existed in Restlawn Memorial Park on Eastern Avenue in Grand Rapids, Michigan. The "Garden of Hope" was developed through a vision to design a garden where post-abortive men and women could go to find comfort and ministry. The focal point of this spiritual park is a bronze sculpture created by nationally acclaimed artist, Beverly Paddleford. The "Hope" piece as it is referred to is a sculpture of Jesus holding an infant, with the baby's mom at Jesus' side.

I went to the "Garden of Hope" specifically to see the sculpture as I had already planned this same scene for this book cover. However, I had not expected what else I found there.

While visiting the park on that rainy July afternoon, Garden of Hope Project Director, Mary Verwys, stood at my side.

My wonderful Christian friend, Larry Claypool, who would become my husband the following year also looked on from a distance. With my umbrella shielding me from the steady rainfall, I bent down to study the names listed on the beautiful monument across from the bronze sculpture. There were only first names, no last names, since these were names of babies who never experienced birth. I was not expecting anything miraculous, I was just curious, and since I was not alone, I was keeping my emotions in check.

I must have audibly gasped when I read the second name on that long list. "Cassandra!" I couldn't believe my eyes, there was Cassie's formal name. I tried to remain calm and detached, when I asked Mary Verwys how the names for the monument had been selected. Her reply was that it was matter of prayer, and trusting God to give them the names that would be significant. Post-abortive women were also contacted and asked if they would like to choose a name for their baby to be placed on the monument.

I will never know how Cassie's name found its way to second place on that list, but I know that ultimately it was God's sovereign hand at work. The Lord touched me in a miraculous way in that moment when I experienced His very personal comfort and forgiveness. He had not only given me a place to find peace, but in His gracious compassion our Heavenly Father had chosen a beautiful garden as my daughter's resting place. I'm so grateful for Cassie's gravesite, but I'm more thankful that she isn't really there. She has found eternal rest in the loving arms of our compassionate Jesus, and one day I will be with her forever.

In the gospel of **Matthew 22:31 & 32**, Jesus himself gives us the reassurance that our children are alive in Him. **"But about the resurrection of the dead — have you not read what God said to you, 'I am the God of Abraham, the God of Isaac, and the God of Jacob?' He is not the God of the dead but of the living."** (NIV)

We opened this book with the Scripture about Rachel's mourning. **"In Rama was there a voice heard, lamentation, and weeping, and great mourning, Rachel weeping for her**

children, and would not be comforted, because they are not."
(Matthew 2:18 KJV)

We close with the promise that the prophet Jeremiah gives to
Rachel. **"Thus saith the Lord: Refrain thy voice from weeping,
and thine eyes from tears: for thy work shall be rewarded,
saith the Lord; and they shall come again from the land of the
enemy. And there is hope in thine end saith the Lord, that thy
children shall come again to their own border."** (Jeremiah 31:16
& 17 KJV)

In order to receive God's comfort you must know His son, Jesus
Christ in a personal way. If you have never accepted the Lord Jesus
into your heart, please pray this prayer aloud:

**Dear Jesus, I need you to be my Lord and my Savior. Please
come into my heart and forgive me of all my sins. Lord, heal
me of my sin, and help me to accept your forgiveness by faith.
I thank you Lord Jesus that you will lead and guide me all the
days of my life. I thank you, too, that I will dwell with you in
Heaven for all eternity in your precious name, Jesus. Amen.**

Dear Father God, thank you so much for the men and women
who have taken time to read this book. Lord, let this be a Rhema
Word in their heart. Help them at all times to choose life.

For those who have committed the sin of abortion, I ask you
to wash them with your blood. Set them free from sin-consciousness and let their minds be renewed in you.

Teach them to understand that although our children cannot
come back to this earth, they are safe with you, waiting for the
great reunion that will occur when we leave this earth.

But for the time we are here, let us not sorrow as the world
sorrows. Let us live with the joy you purchased for each one of us
at the Cross. God heal us spirit, soul, and body. Help us to have
the courage to be a voice against the hideous sin of abortion. Let
us no longer hide the pain that this sin brought into our lives, but
let us shout from the mountaintops warning others. Thank you
Lord, for restoring all that the enemy has taken and for making us
whole in the name of Jesus Christ of Nazareth.

NOTES

Introduction

1) Physicians for Reproductive Choice and Health (PRCH) and the Alan Guttmacher Institute (AGI)*

2) Alan Guttmacher Institute, Facts in Brief. (Jan. 1997) p. 5

3) Physicians for Reproductive Choice and Health (PRCH) and the Alan Guttmacher Institute (AGI)

*Slide and lecture presentation: An Overview of Abortion in the United States. (Jan. 2003) www.guttmacher.org/pubs/ab_slides.html Source: Jones Et al., 2002

4) Alan Guttmacher Institute, Perspectives on Sexual & Reproductive Health Journal. January/Februay 2003

5) The Guttmacher Report on Public policy, Volume 5, Number 3, August 2002, Mifepristone in the United States: Status and Future. Heather Boonstra

* It is important to note that the Alan Guttmacher Institute is an affiliate of pro-choice group Planned Parenthood. The Institute shares board members and financing with Planned Parenthood. However, these secular statistics are a useful indicator of the negative widespread implications that abortion has had on American women and are generally accepted as accurate.

Chapter One — Remembering a Painful Past
Alan Guttmacher Institute, Facts in Brief, Induced Abortion. (Jan. 1997) p.5. *

Chapter Four — The Lie/The Truth
James Strong, The Comprehensive Concordance of the Bible. Iowa Falls, Iowa, World Bible Publishers, Inc., p. 97

Chapter Five — The Laundromat
Anne Sternard, The Unopened Gift. Expressions of Faith, Barbour Publishing, Uhrichsville, Ohio 1998 p. 57 Orig: Guideposts. Carmel, N.Y.

Chapter Six — Forgiven
1) Cesar G. Soriano, Abortion: New Common Ground. USA Weekend, Jan. 9-11, 1998 p. 12

Chapter Ten — Synopsis of the Steps
1) James Strong, The Comprehensive Concordance of the Bible. Iowa Falls, Iowa, World Bible Publishers, Inc., Hebrew and Chaldee Dictionary p. 63
2) Norma McCorvey with Andy Meisler, I Am Roe. Harper Collins Publishers, New York, N.Y. 1994 p. 120
3) Brenda Major, et al., Psychological Responses of Women After First-Trimester Abortions. Archives of General Psychology 57 (August 2000): 777-784
4) Abortion Information Survery, Open Arms National Office, Columbus, MO 1994
5) Hanna Soderberg, et al., "Emotional Distress Following Induced Abortion: A Study of its Incidence and Determinants Among Abortees in Maino, Sweden, "European Journal Obstetrics & Gynecology and Reproductive Biology Vol. 79, No.2 (1998) 173-8
6) Major, Archives of General Psychology, 2000
7) Mika Gissler, et al., "Suicides After Pregnancy in Finland, 1987-94: Register Linkage Study, British Medical Journal 313 (1996): 1431-1434
8) Abortion Information Survery, Open Arms National Office, Columbus, MO 1994
9) Major, Archives of General Psychology, 2000
10) Reardon, et al., "Abortion and Subsequent Substance Abuse," American Journal of Drug and Alcohol Abuse Vol. 26, No 1 (2000) 564-571
11) Centers for Disease Control and Prevention, National Center for Health Statistic, Hyattsville, MD 1996

Chapter Eleven — Telling the World
1) Jeanette Vought, Post-Abortion Trauma. Zondervan Publishing House, Grand Rapids, Michigan 1991

2) Sydna Massé, Her Choice to Heal: Finding Spiritual and Emotional Peace After an Abortion. Ramah International, ramahinternational.org for training seminars
3) Rose Diemler, Starting or Expanding a Post-Abortion Outreach. H.E.A.R.T., Inc.P.O. Box 54783, Cincinnati, OH 45254-0783
4) Norma McCorvey with Gary Thomas, Won By Love. A Janet Thoma Book, Thomas Nelson Publishers, Nashville Tn 1997
5) Cesar G. Sorian, Abortion: New Common Ground. USA Weekend, Jan. 9-11, 1998 p. 12
6) "Ibid.," 12

Chapter 12 — Another Cassie
1) Christina Ryan (Producer), "Jacob's Story - Crack-Addicted Baby," Dr. Vincente Romero, WTLW- TV 44 Feb. 24, 1999
2) "Ibid.,"
3) Sandy Shore, AP, Columbine Victim's Faith Making her a Martyr. The Lima News May 15, 1999
4) "Ibid.,"

ACKNOWLEDGMENTS

Like so many things in the Christian walk it is through the help of others that our vision comes to fruition. In order to publish a book, you need to have other people believe in you, and to also believe in the vision that God has given you. God blessed me with an abundance of self-sacrificing individuals too numerous to name, who assisted in the publication of *Forgiven: finding peace in the aftermath of abortion.*

There are a few people whose effort must be mentioned, as *Forgiven* would have never been published without them. First, I am thankful to my husband Larry Claypool for his constant encouragement and what must have seemed like endless hours of editing. I am also grateful to Larry and my adult son, Zachary Ryan for their willingness to allow me to share shameful moments from my past in order to help those hurting.

Senator Jim Jordan, Dr. John Willke, and State Representative Michael Gilb, I greatly appreciate each of you endorsing this book. Thanks to Ohio Secretary of State J. Kenneth Blackwell for taking time out of your hectic schedule to produce a foreword. Monty Lobb and Mary Sparks your assistance in acting as Mr. Blackwell's liaisons was immeasurable. Thank you to Jon Cross, also!

Dr. Mark Bubeck your willingness and courage to be transparent in the gift of your foreword, and your constant support enabled me to continue this vision in very dark moments.

My editors: Michael Lackey, JoAnne Cramberg, Sean Lause', and Mary Lause' each donated countless hours of editing skills and insight. God truly blessed me with the best and I am so thankful to each of you. Carol Foulkes, your gift of proofreading was greatly appreciated.

My mom Glenna Sprang is an amazing Christian mother who has been an example of God's love and forgiveness. Mom, there is no way I can repay you for your selfless effort in writing Chapter Nine.

122

Thank you to my parents in the faith including: Dr. Ken Copley, Pastor Jerry and Jane Hall, and the late Brother Stan Jacobs for your unceasing prayers on behalf of this vision. Thanks also to Darren Scott for contacting Senator Jordan in reference to an endorsement for this book. "Darren, you went home to be with Jesus way too soon, but I look forward to seeing you on the other side."

Michael and Meg Winkler and Rich and Roz Leahwald, I will be eternally grateful to you for supplying a computer that enabled me to finish this book. Thanks also to John "Ondo" Owens, Jeff Klingler and Bill Fung for your technical computer assistance. David Runk and Renee Shields of CSS Publishing, thank you for your dedication to publishing Christian books of excellence.

My gratitude needs to be extended to Stan Myers for the beautiful artwork and design for the cover of this book. Thanks also to Garden of Hope Project Director, Mary Verwys for her love and support for myself and all post-abortive women and men. My sincere admiration and gratitude to the loving sidewalk counselors, like Mary Verwys, who spend countless hours providing alternatives to the abortion minded.

Special thanks to the men and women of the clergy who have read this book in order to better understand how to minister God's love to those whose lives have been damaged by abortion.

Thanks to each of you who are post-abortive and have been courageous enough to read this book. May God's healing power touch your lives as He has touched mine.

My greatest appreciation is for my Lord and Savior Jesus Christ who has blessed me above all that I could ever ask or imagine.

To schedule Christina for a Speaking Engagement, please write:

Christina Ryan Claypool
New Creation Ministries
P.O. Box 715
Lima, Ohio 45802-0715
www.christinaryanclaypool.com